Smart Management

Smart Management

Using Politics in Organisations

David Butcher

and

Martin Clarke

palgrave

First published 2001 by
PALGRAVE
Houndmills, Basingstoke, Hampshire RG21 6XS and
175 Fifth Avenue, New York, N.Y. 10010
Companies and representatives throughout the world

PALGRAVE is the new global academic imprint of
St. Martin's Press LLC Scholarly and Reference Division and
Palgrave Publishers Ltd (formerly Macmillan Press Ltd).

ISBN 0–333–94903–X hardback

This book is printed on paper suitable for recycling and
made from fully managed and sustained forest sources.

A catalogue record for this book is available
from the British Library.

Library of Congress Cataloging-in-Publication Data has been
applied for.

Editing and origination by
Aardvark Editorial, Mendham, Suffolk

10 9 8 7 6 5 4 3 2 1
10 09 08 07 06 05 04 03 02 01

Printed in and bound in Great Britain by
Creative Print & Design (Wales), Ebbw Vale

Contents

List of Figures

Acknowledgements

We would like to thank our colleagues Catherine Bailey, Mike Meldrum, Sally Atkinson, Judy Merrick, Dawn Paterson, Kiarin Oosthuizen, Justine Johnson, Juliette Lee and Lianne Robinson for helping to create the environment in which this book could be successfully completed.

Every effort has been made to trace all the copyright holders but if any have been inadvertently overlooked the publishers will be pleased to make the necessary arrangements at the first opportunity.

Preface

A glance at the titles along the bookshelves, or in the catalogue from which you may have selected this book, might leave you with the impression that over the last few years every fundamental principle of managing and organising has come under the microscope. Confronted with an endless array of potential arrangements for managing customers, suppliers, partners and employees, you could be forgiven for thinking that management can no longer take anything for granted. There is now, more than ever before, a plethora of possibilities for managers to choose from in their quest to create and sustain effective organisations of every kind.

So have these sea changes in the business landscape led to fundamentally different ways of organising and managing? After all we now talk of empowerment and organisational citizenship as routinely as we might have talked of corporate planning and employee loyalty 20 years ago. But when we strip away the rhetoric has anything really changed about our notion of organisations? Many people think so. Sumantra Ghoshal, one of today's leading management thinkers, puts it this way:[1]

> Companies are trying to implement their sophisticated, multidimensional third generation strategies, through their de-layered, horizontal, second generation organisations – but they are still trying to do that with first generation managers – managers whose personal sense of their roles and value added, and whose personal skills and competencies, have all been shaped by an earlier, outdated model.

This outdated model is one in which hierarchical authority structures still greatly influence managerial thought in practice. Just imagine, for example, that you have been away from your office for a day, and you have returned to find three e-mails. One is from a colleague, one from your team and one from your boss. Each is marked urgent, but there is no other detail. Which do you respond to first? You probably won't ponder the answer for too long. Or consider how easy it is to challenge established procedures, or question a change inspired by the board without this becoming career limiting. Organisations may have become delayered and flattened, but the role of hierarchy and authority still runs deep in managerial minds. Of course hierarchy is inevitable in any form of organising, but it is the way it obscures the value of a different perspective on managing that has prompted us to write this book.

For many years management theorists have discussed the idea that organisations are akin to groups of competing and mutual interest groups that sometimes come together to produce something worthwhile. They are seldom uniform undertakings of rational, hierarchical co-ordination and action. Instead, agendas constantly collide and align around different issues, and managers spend most of their time dealing with this. It is the stuff of politics and managers, whether we like it or not, are politicians.

Many managers understand this of course. They experience it every day, but this insight has never been allowed to develop in a way that can help them understand its centrality to what they do, or how they can use it for personal and organisational benefit. Instead, organisational politics are treated as illegitimate or, at best, with superficial understanding. As if to make this point for us, a recent article in a US management journal described political skill as 'disarmingly charming' behaviour. Another piece in the same issue talked of office politics becoming temporarily suspended when there is a hot job market and increasing economic prosperity. These kinds of misconception are naïve and can seriously mislead managers as to the real nature of organisational politics.

The record needs to be put straight. Management is politics. It is our own view that the illegitimacy of organisational politics is one of the major reasons why third generation strategies are still being implemented with first generation managers. Many managers still feel uncomfortable about challenging the top-down corporatist mindset. For if politics are perceived as illegitimate in organisational terms, then how can alternative views be acceptable? We ourselves believe that ideas such as organisational citizenship and empowerment are more rhetorical than real, and will remain so until managers are able to get to grips with the inevitable pluralism of organisational life. With this uppermost in our minds, we hope that this book challenges your notions of organising and managing, and allows you to develop new and practical ways of meeting your own personal goals in the best interests of the organisation for which you work.

DAVID BUTCHER AND MARTIN CLARKE
Cranfield School of Management, UK

---

1. Sumantra, Ghoshal (1997) *European Management Journal*, December **15**(6),626

List of Abbreviations

BULs   business unit leaders

CEO   chief executive officer

HR   human resources

HRM   human resource management

IRA   Irish Republican Army

IS   information systems

IT   information technology

MD   managing director

MNC   multinational corporation

MRP2   manufacturing and resources planning

SAP   systems applications and products

VP   vice-president

CHAPTER 1

Organisational Politics

We are writers and practitioners in the field of management and organisation development. Over the last five years we have had the opportunity to work, or at least talk, in depth with perhaps as many as 5000 managers. These managers have come from all the continents of the world, from a very broad array of backgrounds and cultures, industries and jobs. Our relationship with them arises because, by and large, they are all looking for answers to what they consider to be difficult, and sometimes intractable, management problems. They can easily appear to be confused, disillusioned and disempowered, sometimes unrealistically confident and buoyant, but they almost always seem to be looking for models, tools and techniques to make their managerial and leadership roles easier and more fulfilling. It is not that they expect us to provide definitive answers. After all, they are usually experienced, thinking people who know that organisations are too complex to be reduced to simple recipes for solving all managerial problems. No – it is as though there is a piece of the organisational jigsaw puzzle missing, something that they are not taking account of, a core assumption they are making that does not hold.

We run up against this with so many managers we encounter that it has left us thinking again and again about this 'missing

1

link'. Why does the accumulated knowledge of organisational best practice and the science of managerial decision-making fail them so consistently? We keep coming back to this question, especially when we find ourselves talking to successful executives who seem to be doing all the right things, *and* have had the opportunity of extensive management training and development. The case of Dan provides a representative example.

Dan is the local UK managing director of a predominately US-based business in a globally branded organisation. On the face of it, he felt he was doing rather well. In less than 12 months he had reduced the cost profile and refocused the business towards its most profitable markets. In fact the business was making more money under his guidance than it had done in the last four years. Yet despite this, he had received feedback from his US boss that he needed to be more strategic. Dan was annoyed by this view because he had made several proposals to the executive board to acquire some complementary e-business companies, but these had been turned down. He was also receiving feedback from senior management that his staff were concerned about his management style. Here again he was disappointed because his annual 360-degree appraisal indicated that staff morale was good. His boss also criticised him for not working more collaboratively with the other business units, despite the fact he was always telling his team to talk to these people. Evidently they weren't. As a result of all this Dan was confused. If he needed any help at all, he thought, it would come from exposure to some new ideas on strategy, getting in touch with the latest thinking ... but then again, he reasoned, he had only recently been on a leadership programme at a top US business school.

This case is not unique; it reflects themes that we encounter every week in every management situation. Contradictory feedback, confused strategic focus and poor interpersonal relationships are but a few of these. And so we are confronted with the question of why.

To judge from the amount that is written about 'the changing face of business' you could be forgiven for thinking that the answer should be obvious by now. Pick up any journal aimed at practising managers. You will read of more new techniques, best practice breakthroughs, and world-class organisations that are apparently resolving these issues through 'millennium strategy workshops', new competency frameworks, in-house leadership development programmes, or 'master classes' at corporate universities. There is no shortage of remedies for the sick business, all of which are offered against the backdrop of the need for organisational transformation as the new economy advances.

Globalisation, technological advances and rampant competition, it is argued, are the driving forces, and they are clearly very real. But is this really resulting in a basic shift in assumptions about the essential ingredients of organisation and the fundamentals of management? The new economy business paradigm says 'yes'. It is supposedly clearing away the flotsam of old organisation thinking, and throughout the 1990s we were told that agility, constant innovation, collaboration and chaos are the future. This means that, in theory, managers are turning into flexible knowledge workers who network, build portfolio careers and who achieve a healthy work–life balance. So when they complain that 'we don't have a clear business strategy', 'I don't know what I'm supposed to be doing', 'I'm asked to do contradictory things by different people', 'my boss never gives me enough resource', or 'I never get to see the kids enough', it is very tempting to see these problems as simply part of an inevitable transition towards a different way of working. Except for one thing – they are not new complaints. They can certainly be traced as management development and organisational improvement themes over the past 40 years, probably much longer. And so we are left with the inconvenient but intriguing possibility that they are indicative of a more

deep-seated organisational dilemma that extends well beyond the move to a new economy.

This is what interests us. Organisations appear to be constantly changing yet something is clearly staying the same. Something is distorting or at least filtering the momentum of continual change on contemporary organisations. That something is what we have come to describe as the *rational mindset*. It is set deep in the foundations of organisational architecture but can be observed in the rhetoric that companies use to enforce their vision and values. It can be seen in the way that organisational culture change programmes push for unrealistic levels of collaboration, and how formal authority is sometimes misused to quash dissension and conflict. More importantly, it can obscure the role of individual self-interest and action in actually bringing about change. Or to use another phrase, it can suppress the role of *organisational politics* as a key component of managerial activity. We believe that it is the long-standing interplay between the rational mindset and organisational politics that lies at the heart of what we are seeing. Organisational politics represents the missing link, and drawing attention to it as central to managerial work is the aim of this book. More exactly, the book is a practical guide for managers on how to work with both the rationality that is expected of them, and the inevitable self-interest they see in themselves and others, which it makes little sense to deny. It is a book about how to use all that is good about politics, and to do so with skill and a clear conscience.

In this, the first chapter we will set out that proposition for you, the reader, in more detail. We will briefly examine some of the issues facing organisations today and how they are trying to meet these challenges. This 'change management focus' will enable us to explore the endemic nature of the rational mindset, and its influence on companies as they try to readjust to the demands of the twenty-first-century business environment. It will then be easier to see how, in consequence, organisational politics have been largely seen as a major block to meeting these challenges. The rest of the chapter will explore why politics are important and a potentially positive force, and how this book will reframe the

use of power and politics in organisational life as a valuable missing discipline of effective management.

All Change!

There is now common agreement about how quickly the world is changing. A few years ago, one of the leading consultancies produced a statement to the effect that by the time someone born today reaches the age of 21, everything known in the world will have doubled. Of course, this wildly intuitive idea cannot be proven, but the sentiment provides an interesting insight into how people are now thinking about the pace of change. Not surprisingly, the 'business and management' displays in airport bookstores bulge with offerings from authors keen to explain to us how these seismic shifts in the tectonics of business are affecting corporate strategy. It is not our intention to replicate any of this analysis in detail here, but a summary of the main considerations can be found below. Suffice to say that the significance of these huge and emerging changes has been, and will continue to be, the subject of conversations in boardrooms, cafeteria, corridors and conference halls throughout the business world.

Some of the Significant Drivers of Business Change

The Impact of Technological Advances

- E-business: increasing the depth and breadth of access to markets, and individual customers, enhancing co-ordination with supplier, the growth of 'infomediaries', fragmentation of businesses into smaller entrepreneurial organisational forms.

- Communication: linking PC and non-PC products, increasing the speed of decision-making and changing where work is carried out, enhancing the co-ordination of dispersed activities.

- Production processes: automation, driving down costs and streamlining processes.

- Biotechnology: creation of new markets.

- Reducing the opportunity for long-term competitive advantage: the early maturation and saturation of markets, early redundancy of plant and equipment, increasing the need for innovation.

The Drive for Innovation

- The opportunity to achieve mass customisation: explosion of customer choice, the increasing power of buyers, customers designing their own products.

- Investment and exploitation in organisational knowledge: empowering individuals to apply their knowledge closer to the customer, attracting and retaining innovative talent, an increased investment in R&D.

- The learning company: establishing looser more fluid organisational forms and working environments to facilitate continual learning and creativity.

The Impact of Globalisation

- Convergence of business practices: disproportionate influence of multinational corporations (MNCs) on the

world economy, the impact of government and the trend toward deregulation, the 'westernisation' of business and business practices, emergence of global brands.

■ Easier access to markets and increased competition: the importance of global supply chain management and logistics, shifting production centres to exploit cheaper labour.

■ Developing international mindsets: changing managerial work patterns, identifying and developing expatriate management and international leaders, working around time zones, across borders and in virtual teams.

The Concern for Business Ethics

■ The socially responsible management of organisations: the impact of organisations on the environment, concern for gender and racial equality, the growth in socially responsible investment.

■ The role of organisations in society: the impact of the values of MNCs in Third World countries.

■ People as an organisation's greatest asset: the development of 'human capital', the increasing importance of human resource policy, promoting work–life balance.

The consensus that has been emerging from these discussions over the last few years indicates that these changes are expected to influence the nature and experience of all aspects of business and organisational life. A business paradigm is emerging in which organisations have less well-defined boundaries, and are

in practice highly interdependent with other organisations in the supply chain or 'industry set'. Companies are 'unbundling' themselves from unprofitable business legacies and concentrating on leveraging core competencies that are the source of sustainable competitive advantage. Consequently, more than ever, it is said, corporations will rely on the power of inspirational leadership to produce a unity of purpose among highly employable individuals who can take their intellectual property elsewhere. As this new business paradigm gathers momentum, those employees will become 'citizens' in organisational communities, in which the strategic value of individual know-how will ensure that people are accorded the autonomy and respect they desire and deserve. Organisations will therefore place a premium on stimulating innovation, and on staff sharing their tacit knowledge in high performing and collaborative teams. More and more people will have the opportunity to tele-work, restoring their work–life balance, and companies will be genuinely concerned to develop people as individuals, not as 'heads', 'hands' or 'human resources'. Familiar scenario building?

Some of these shifts are already with us and some may or may not transpire in reality. That is in the nature of predictions about future scenarios. And because the changes are global and all embracing, they are by definition on an unprecedented scale. It is therefore understandable to argue that they make demands which managers are not used to, and will struggle to understand. Who can be blamed for feeling confused and displaced in such circumstance? Not only that, but if organisations struggle to adjust, surely that too is entirely understandable.

It is a seductive line of reasoning, but at the same time it obscures a key question. Does the novelty and scale of the changes truly explain the high degrees of uncertainty and scepticism apparently experienced by managers? After all, some of these shifts have been troubling business for some time. Consider, for example, the idea of people finally emerging as an organisation's 'greatest asset'. That has been a feature of the business landscape for at least the last 30 years. Similarly the power of visionary leadership and high performing teams has

been core curriculum for management development programmes since the 1970s. The same can be said of the need to stimulate organisational innovation or about the importance of reducing working hours.

Clearly, organisations have found these kinds of changes extremely difficult to introduce. Even today, the number of organisations that reflect these qualities in depth and breadth are few – too few to describe as a sea change in business attitudes and values. What is more, the many management journals that report the breakthroughs in management practice in these companies are equally liberally sprinkled with studies that reveal rising levels of employee stress fuelled by:

■ People's day-to-day experience of organisational life; inadequate communication, limited participation, discourteous treatment, management incompetence, racial and gender discrimination, and the use of management fads

■ Individual job/role frustrations; role ambiguity, role conflict and work overload

■ Reports of organisational injustice in terms of higher executive pay, harsh layoffs, unjustified corporate profits and corporate irresponsibility.

It is a catalogue of problems that brings us right back to what interests us most. Why are employees still reporting these kinds of issues at a time when such concerns are supposed to be resolved through new organisational forms and working patterns? Our answer is the deep-seated influence of a *rational mindset* on managerial thinking. It pervades all aspects of organisational activity from team working to strategy development. It is central to what organisations are supposed to be: ordered groups of people working collaboratively towards a common goal or strategy. And inevitably, therefore, it provides the guiding principles for managing organisational change itself, which in turn has a fundamental consequence. Many rationally

driven change management processes simultaneously build new
difficulties into the transformations they are there to facilitate.
For that reason the conventions of change management provide a
very useful way of illustrating what the rational mindset means
in practice, exposing some of the key values and ideas upon
which it is built. Let us briefly focus on this change management
theme to see what it can reveal about the rational mindset.

The Nature of the Problem

In the rational model of management, organisations are
supposed to be places of corporate unity in which all employees
work with consistent strategies cascaded down through the
various levels and processes of the organisation. This is a
common sense basis for efficient and effective working. So
when change is perceived as necessary, usually by senior
management, the outmoded way of working is substituted for
another, more effective one. Conventions of change management, therefore, have been built on the logic of consistent top-
down processes that establish conformity and control in the
wider interest of efficiency. Direction is provided from the top
(see Figure 1.1) and backed by vision and value statements that
reflect strong judgements about acceptable behaviours which, in
turn, implicitly discourage dissension from that vision. Participation and consultation are generally only permitted within this
framework. Once employees appreciate the rational logic of
collaboratively working towards common goals, it is believed,
they will share their organisational knowledge in the wider
interests of the enterprise.

We caricature the 'rationality' of top-down change to illustrate
a basic point. Even when these principles are overlaid with the
impression that participation and involvement is a central pillar
of good practice (as with senior management-led question and
answer sessions, or focus groups), change processes never seem
to actually run this way in reality. More often than not the

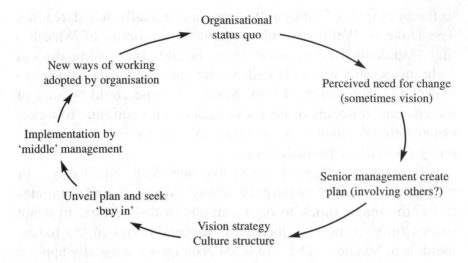

Figure 1.1 The theory of planned change

required change falters on issues of personal power and self-interest, becoming remoulded and reinterpreted. Yet despite this, and the reality of the wholesale changes facing organisations, these basic principles have formed the centrepiece of change management for many years.

There is a now a burgeoning body of opinion in Europe and the US from academics and practitioners alike, that top-down processes of change actually undermine the chance of stimulating the empowerment and motivation that they seek to instil. Study after study reveals employees from the top to the bottom of companies who have become frustrated, stressed and disempowered by processes of organisation change that are designed to unleash their potential, not diminish it. Despite this evidence, 'thought leaders' on the new economy still promulgate the notion that vision and corporate higher purpose provide the essential point of stability and motivational framework, thereby enabling employees to commit their hearts and minds to an organisation. Above all what this ignores is the self-interest and partisan mentality that is not only inherent in organisations, but if seen as destructive, becomes just that. Unwavering adherence

to the principles of rationality, then, is eventually self-defeating. The Duke of Wellington observed after the battle of Waterloo that Napoleon tried to advance in the old style, using the old techniques, and was defeated by the same defensive response that had always defeated him. Much the same could be said of the change strategies of business leaders who continue to tackle organisational renewal from a rational perspective, without due recognition of its intrinsic flaws.

It is our belief that this pervasive and deep-seated drive for rationality and unity of purpose, always has been, and continues to be, the major block to organisations in their efforts to adapt successfully to the ever-increasing discontinuities in the fundamentals of business. These rational principles are usually applied with the very best of intentions but without a full recognition of the impact they have on the behaviour of organisational members. This is not to do with the value of rationality itself or with the idea of hierarchy; these two concepts are fundamental to all organising. No, the problem lies in the unknowing and indiscriminate application of these ideas, implicitly undermining alternative viewpoints and hence the value of constructive self-interest in creating organisational improvements. For example, Motorola, a global company of over 135,000 employees, used to have a compensation and benefits strategy based on exporting US ideas to the rest of the corporation. This included an incentive programme that awarded Motorola stock for high performance. This meant cascading the principles of the US scheme across many different cultures and legal frameworks. The result was a hugely expensive white elephant. Stock options were not considered as worthwhile incentives in many Motorola operations and they eventually discovered that in the Philippines, for example, employees valued different benefits like a weekly five-pound bag of rice. This is a simple example, but illustrates the difficulty of factoring local interests and alternative views into a rational and hierarchical mindset.

It is our contention that self-interest and the alternative viewpoints that it generates are fundamentally important for the effective working of organisations in the future.

This understanding is based on the reality that organisations cannot be places of unity. As in Motorola, individuals bring their personal interests and aspirations to the workplace with them, and these are not usually easily reconciled to concerns about shareholder value and economic value-add. This plurality of interests is therefore equally as important and implicit as rationality in the management of organisations. Having come to this recognition, it is axiomatic to acknowledge that organisations are essentially all about politics. In reality, managers are engaged in a ceaseless process of dealing with these differences, of positioning their own interests in relation to those of others, including the organisational change agendas of top executives. And of course, reconciling alternative viewpoints is what politics are all about.

Most seasoned managers readily acknowledge this because coping with competing interests is routine experience for them. It is not a new element in managerial work, and therein lies a fundamental problem. The rational organisational mindset has always defined plurality of interests in general, and self-interest in particular, as illegitimate. 'Constructive politics' is a contradiction in terms for many managers – as a principle of organisation it certainly does not enjoy equal status with rational decision-making as an official or rightful means of working through differences. Perhaps the tremendous pace of change is only now revealing to us the central nature of politics in organisations, and the value of constructively using mutual and competing interests for individual and organisational benefit. So what has been holding us back from seeing this, and what do we need to do to reframe organisational politics so that they can be used for productive purpose?

Politics is a Dirty Word

Perhaps the biggest difficulty in seeing the constructive value of organisational politics is the reputation they have. The common

perception of politics is well summarised by Beverly Stone in her book *Confronting Company Politics*:[1]

> The term company politics refers to all the game-playing, snide, them and us, aggressive, sabotaging, negative, blaming, win–lose, with-holding, non-co-operative behaviour that goes on in hundreds of inter-actions every day in your organisation. Those who indulge in company politics do so in order to achieve their personal agenda at the expense of others in the organisation. In the process, they demoralise the motivated and sabotage the company's success. Given their limited numbers, like one or two bad apples souring the whole barrel, they are disproportion-ately powerful.

This highly judgemental description is interesting because it embodies many popular assumptions about politics. First, it suggests that politics are seen to be entirely concerned with div-isive self-interest and personal agenda. The implication here is that self-interest cannot be positive and is, by definition, bound to 'sabotage the company's success'. Second, it is only a few 'bad apples' who 'indulge' in politics – 'politics', therefore, represent something that others do to us rather than something endemic to managing. Furthermore, politics are by definition 'non-co-operative', which of course runs counter to the idea that political processes are concerned with respecting differences. With value judgements like these it is hardly surprising that 'politics' has come to be seen as a dirty word.

We can also see in this description the power of the rational mindset in undermining the potentially positive aspects of polit-ical activity. Many of Beverly Stone's propositions are clearly based on the rational values of collaboration, unity and consensus. The stronger the influence of the rational model, the weaker the proposition for constructive politics becomes. Because the influence of the rational model is generally so deeply felt in assumptions about the nature of management itself, appreciating the value of alternative approaches can be extremely difficult. Take the following example:

A number of managers attending a workshop investi-
gating new approaches to teamwork were debating the
problems of really getting people to co-operate effectively together. They believed that conventional team
development failed to get to grips with the stresses and
demands of increasingly ambiguous job roles and
complex organisation structures. They also recognised
that some of the values underlying the idea of teamwork, such as trust and collaboration, were often unat-
tainable or took too much effort to create. They went so
far as to recognise that individuals have motives and
goals that often conflict with company policy, and
therefore getting a team to commit exclusively to a
common goal without acknowledging the importance of
personal agendas may be pointless. The group then
turned their attention to considering what should be
done to use teams more effectively. Their responses
came straight from the pages of the rational textbook.
They decided that more effort needed to be put into
establishing clear goals, roles and strong leadership, and
that greater priority needed to be given to creating clear
procedures and performance measures that closely
reflected organisational strategy. In the end, they had
created a set of recommendations that was largely indis-
tinguishable from the best practice advice they had
believed not to work in the first place. They had become
trapped in the logic of rational management.

This rational view is reinforced time and time again. Earlier we
used the example of top-down change initiatives to reveal the
workings of the rational mindset, but it is crucial to emphasise
that its reach is to be felt in all forms of management and organisational activities. We see it, for instance, in centralised human

resources (HR) policy that seeks to instil common behaviours, or in appraisal systems based on the notion that people can be assessed on 'objective' criteria unsullied by personal views. It is embedded in the language we use to create business strategy – words and phrases such as 'mission' and 'strategic intent' reflect a sense of unity and control. Against the strength of these images it is little wonder that some managers find it hard to see any alternatives at all.

Organisational politics are also sometimes equated with the seamier side of governmental politics. For many, parliamentary politics are increasingly focused on adversarial battles and broken promises, while the pursuit of power is often seen to be an end in itself. These images are just too powerful not to spill over into parallels with organisational life where formal authority is similarly often seen to be abused for personal gain. This perspective is amply demonstrated by the results of a survey undertaken by the authors among senior managers from a diverse range of organisations, who had all embarked on substantial change initiatives.

The managers were asked questions about how they introduced their changes, what resistance and co-operation they experienced and how this was managed. Well over half of the survey reported that key decision-makers and bosses were resistant to the ideas put forward by the managers. In 44 per cent of these cases, formal authority was used to block the ideas, rather than good logical argument, powerful role modelling or even subtle reward. Just old-fashioned 'I'm the boss', with no further explanation offered. The interpretations placed on this resistance from decision-makers by those introducing the change were very revealing. To them, the underlying causes were to do with personal self-interest reflected in concerns for loss of control, challenge to

personal competence, and loss of face and status. Furthermore, nearly half of those resisting were covert in this, choosing to be 'economical with the truth' about their real concerns.

It is not surprising therefore, to find managers using words such as secrecy, lobbying and spin to describe both organisational and governmental politics alike. Even in academic circles, where such emotive descriptions should be replaced with analytical enquiry, politics have been viewed as an 'ugly duckling', 'a distasteful but persistent phenomenon' and an 'irrational intrusion'. Certainly, many academics recognise the pluralistic nature of organisations, but nevertheless, in standard texts on organisational behaviour, politics usually only warrant a sub-heading in a chapter on power and conflict. Cast as but another aspect of organisational life to be considered by the student of human behaviour, the centrality and role of politics are obscured and marginalised.

This lack of a consistent academic approach to the subject, together with the power of the rational model to cast dissension in a destructive light, and the unhelpful comparisons with governmental politics, have created a negative interpretation of the potential value of political activity in organisations. Inevitably, therefore, our first task in this book is to try and recast politics in a more favourable light. Interestingly, our survey provided a glimpse of how powerful a constructive political perspective can be. After around six months of implementing change, 80 per cent of the managers reported that their greater awareness of self-interest was of direct use in effectively managing their boss and other key decision-makers. Furthermore, they felt that their own acceptance of the inevitability of political motives was crucial to the success of their change projects. No less than 95 per cent saw the need to manage political behaviour as central to the task of managing change.

A Powerful Alternative

The individuals who took part in this survey were a small sample of the many managers with whom we have worked over the last five years. Much of this work has concentrated on enabling them to take a much more critical perspective of the rational model and of the value of constructive political action. Our work with them is based on four core ideas, and they form the basis for this book. These ideas are appropriate at any level of management, and we have seen them successfully applied in many different cultures, countries and industries because they are inseparable from the process of managing itself.

The Centrality of Politics to Organisations and Managing

First, we ask you to think of organisational politics as central to all significant organisational activity. If organisations are more realistically perceived as collections of competing and mutual interest groups, then politics, the process through which these differing perspectives are reconciled, is the way that change is realised, strategy formulated and so on. *We therefore define politics as those deliberate efforts made by individuals and groups in organisations to use power in pursuit of their own particular interests.* Because vested interests are part and parcel of managing, managers are in effect engaged in a continual process of political positioning. This involves them influencing in ways that are not seen as part of the 'official' range of managerial activities – lobbying and behind the scenes alliance-building, for example.

For those of a rational persuasion it is tempting to see words like lobbying and positioning, and interpret them from a rational standpoint. Of course, such activities are a necessary part of management, whatever perspective one uses, but they take on a different hue when working from a political perspective. For those who understand the centrality of politics to organising,

such activities *represent the task of management*, as opposed to being something that managers *sometimes have to do*, reluctantly and even against their better judgement.

Understanding the centrality of politics to managing is the foundation for recognising personal interests as a way of unleashing energy and motivation to get things achieved. Political activity, far from 'sabotaging company success', offers the opportunity to build on mutual and competing interests for the long-term benefit of the organisation. This assertion is based on the simple truism that individuals are much more likely to be motivated to make things happen when they can see a personal relevance for doing so. In the rational model of top-down change, personal relevance is often too far removed to be of real consequence. Corporate higher purpose has never been sufficient to engage everyone at the same time in an organisation. It is less likely still to sustain the motivation and commitment required to make things happen in fast moving and pressurised organisations. Furthermore, well-intentioned ideas that are in opposition to one another can be an asset, not a liability. They can create productive conflict that stimulates innovation, 'thinking outside of the box' and so on. Reframed in this way, managing competing interests is critical for organisations to be able to reinvent themselves constantly in the face of furious environmental change, as we are told they need to do.

The Principled Use of Power

At first sight, this idea may seem unduly positive or even naïve; there is a fine line between the use and abuse of power, and managers are always familiar with the dangers of uncoupling power and politics from an ethical framework. The single-minded pursuit of power through political means has been with us since Machiavelli, and the idea that managers should seek to extend their personal power in pursuit of vested interests therefore requires a robust justification on our part.

How, then, can the negative aspects of personal agendas and potential abuse of power be managed? Can there be effective political behaviour without it inevitably becoming deceitful and underhand? The answer to these questions lies in generating a clear understanding of the relationship between power, the ability to influence others, and the political process itself. Ironically, given the widespread scepticism about the nature of modern democratic government, it is that which provides a model for us to understand how power can be used in the long-term interests of others. In the realms of government, politics in theory represent the battle of just causes. So long as causes are principled, and in the interests of others, there is no issue over the legitimacy of the activity of politics itself. A news item on BBC radio in May 2000 provides a helpful illustration of the potency of this idea.

The item reported that David Trimble, the leader of the Ulster Unionists in Northern Ireland, had postponed a meeting of the Unionists for a week so that he was able to build support for the latest peace proposal by the IRA. Here is governmental politics in the raw – overt lobbying to position a secular cause of the utmost gravity. But, the central point here is that no one doubted David Trimble's motives. Even those opposed to his position could not doubt that he was acting on a principled cause, even if that principle was seen as detrimental to their own interests.

There is an important parallel here with business. Managers delay meetings to build support and they have to make judgements about how open to be about their intentions. Their reasons may sometimes be less transparent than in the world of government, but that in itself need not make them any less principled. However, the process they use does not enjoy the same authenticity in organisational terms as it does in government. We will explore these issues as we proceed in order to show that once political positioning is seen as a legitimate managerial activity, the problem of personal motives diminishes.

Balancing Individual and Organisational Motives

Of course, for the Ulster Unionists, the causes and their princi-ples are clear and well articulated. In the daily 'to and fro' of organisational politics the principles will be more opaque. One person's just cause may be another's reduced headcount, and in such circumstances, who defines what is 'in the best interests of the organisation'? After all, it is possible to produce an organ-isational justification for almost any kind of action, even for the most blatant of self-serving agendas. So, central to the idea of principled political action is the need for individuals to achieve a balance between self-interest, and action in the interests of others. Constructive politicians need to be able to create a mean-ingful justification for their agendas. It must be built on a clear understanding of the key business issues to be tackled as they see them, and on how progress with these will be enabled through influential relationships.

For any one of us that is difficult to achieve, and there are considerable implications for the development and capabilities of managers. Being able to balance motives in this way is not simply achieved by the acquisition of new managerial knowledge, concepts and frameworks. It requires a substantial commitment to learning that enhances personal and interpersonal awareness, so as to be able to understand well the motivations of oneself and others. It demands a critical perspective on what really makes organisations work, so as to see beyond the superficial aspects of the rational model. It implies a reconsideration of personal atti-tudes to conflict, integrity and the responsible use of power. And so, because this may be a personal transition of some magnitude, we will consider it in depth, showing the reader a practical route to becoming a constructive politician.

The Redefinition of Managerial Work

This transition causes us to question the nature of what managers actually do. In effect, a constructive political mindset redefines

the basics of day-to-day managerial activity because it focuses attention on the precarious way that the taken-for-granted essentials – rules, roles, procedures and accountabilities – are held in place. For example, in the rational model, decision-making is largely a function of hierarchy. Even in the flattest of companies, managers are given different levels of authority for that very purpose. However, politically able managers are much more critical of rational processes of corporate decision-making. They understand well that power is not always congruent with formal authority, and strategic decisions can sometimes be made informally, irrespective of that authority. Politically able managers are therefore much more aware of the opportunity to make initiatives happen regardless of accepted ways of working. This necessitates developing a range of influential organisational relationships, up, down, sideways and external to the organisation. Such a network provides them with the base from which to stay tuned to emergent issues, lobby for support, test out the value of different projects, and so forth.

The recognition that organisational strategies and initiatives emerge from negotiations between parties with vested interests has significant impact on where managers spend their time and energy. For example, politically capable managers often give priority to building change from the bottom-up, through local initiatives. Sometimes these initiatives run counter to official policy and are accomplished only through the use of power and political stealth. But in all cases, such initiatives are motivated by individuals who are prepared to take responsibility to make things happen because they can see a personal relevance of doing so. And it implies managerial activity patterns that cut right across the normal focus on consistency, control and collaboration.

In Conclusion

These four core ideas will be used as building blocks to develop a practical guide to managing in contemporary organisations. Many

books are long on advice about how to re-engineer organisations to ride the waves of change, but short on practical guidance for individual managers wishing to realise these new ways of working. This book, in contrast, has been written with a strong personal development focus. We hope it will act as a mirror in which managers can examine their own reflections. Together with the analysis of organisations as both rational and political realms of activity, there are many case histories, role analyses and anecdotes culled from real life managerial experiences. They are there so that the reader can make comparisons with his or her own managerial work and organisational circumstances. Our intention is that the book will provide a platform from which to develop greater personal influence and managerial effectiveness.

Our aim is to encourage reflection, not only on assumptions about managerial work, but also on the wider implications of a political mindset for organisational effectiveness. Indeed, towards the end of this book we will suggest that, so far-reaching are the ramifications of 'legitimate' organisational politics, that they prompt questions about the future form of organisations, the nature of power relationships within them, and the impact of organisations on society at large. Our conclusion is that in the long term, acknowledging the importance of politics is critical for the successful establishment of the much heralded new economy. But more of that later.

Politics then, are much, much more than the negative by-product of the 'personal agendas' described by Beverly Stone. That said, there are limits to the value of organisational politics, principally the need for rationality. The two will continue to coexist. However, the ability to see through the dysfunctional elements of the rational mindset can be a great emancipation for managers. Constructive political activity provides opportunities to make things happen as individuals and groups in a way that enhances personal freedom, choice and autonomy. And, of course, organisational effectiveness.

---

1. Stone, Beverley (1997) *Confronting Company Politics*, Macmillan – now Palgrave

CHAPTER 2

The Illegitimacy
of Politics

This chapter will explore in more detail why politics is such a dominant organisational feature. We will begin by exploring the different mindsets that managers form about the world in which they work. These make an important contribution to the way managers interpret their organisational roles, and our purpose, of course, will be to highlight politics as a highly significant mindset. We will show how this both fits and jars with the 'official' mindset – that of rational hierarchy.

The idea of mindsets will help us examine why managers come to see political action as illegitimate. This will include an exploration of some of the inherent contradictions of the official rational model, and how these contradictions can hinder top management's attempts to 'decorporatise' organisations. It will also examine how some of the more significant downsides of this hierarchical mindset create an environment in which political activity is seen as negative. These negative consequences arise from a drive for an unrealistic level of organisational co-ordination, and sometimes from well intentioned but vague notions of trust and openness. Each creates strong negative judgements about the role of self-interest in managerial action. For example, the idea of corporate unity, reflected in mission and value statements, is deeply embedded in most organisations. Yet,

in reality, it is a myth – it does not exist precisely because of the inevitability of political self-interest. Such strong organisational assumptions make it difficult for managers to see the constructive value of political action.

In the rest of the chapter we will reframe the political mindset by examining its constructive contribution in helping managers make more of a difference to their organisations, one that they might otherwise see to be beyond their influence. For example, as managers come to view their organisations as collections of competing interest groups, they also see the relevance of individual power and self-determination. They achieve more because they are not limited to the official mindset of rational top-down control. Analysing what really happens in organisations by using a political mindset allows managers to take a much more critical approach to their work, to challenge assumptions, initiate change, and above all, get results.

Managerial Mindsets

We saw in the first chapter that political action is entirely endemic to managerial life; it is the very essence of what managers do, but is often seen as peripheral. It is more likely to be viewed as an aberration than as a means for getting results. Why, then, should there be such a *tension* between the reality of political activity and how managers feel about it? To understand this tension it is first necessary to understand how managers come to see the organisations in which they work.

Organisations today are complex and serve a multiplicity of purposes. In consequence, there are many different ways in which managers can view their work. For example, an organisation can be seen as a means of providing employment, creating wealth for shareholders, supplying important services to local communities, or as the context for individual identity formation and fulfilment. These different purposes evolve over time into what are often known as mindsets. It is a complex

process that sometimes runs through society as a whole, contributed to by business leaders and high profile opinion-makers, the media, educational and professional institutions and many other influences. Once an organisational mindset has taken root it is reinforced through everyday behaviour and the language used to describe organisational experiences. In simple terms a mindset is a particular way of thinking about day-to-day experience which makes it hard to understand how other perspectives could have equal or greater merit. We can have a strong mindset about the nature of the organisations in which we work, as we obviously do about family life, professional practice or sportsmanship. The mindset encourages us to define implicitly what is appropriate and inappropriate in each of these circumstances. In the context of management it serves the purpose of helping us to decide what is best practice, and to understand the essential nature of organisations. And as one would expect, the stronger the mindset, the more deeply it influences how managers view their roles because it is a means of both interpreting and evaluating thc world.

There is rarely only one mindset associated with a particular institution or realm of social activity. For example, there are many associated with the family, particularly when we make comparisons across cultures. Organisations are no exception to this, and it is possible to recognise a number of generic mindsets, each of which exerts influence for some people. Take, for example, the economist's view of organisations, often strikingly portrayed in news bulletins. In this mindset, organisations are seen to have little independence because they are apparently at the whim of interest and exchange rates, market forces, government action and a host of other factors. In the extreme, organisations become like black boxes where what goes on inside does not really matter – the contribution of management to any one firm becomes, therefore, largely irrelevant. Choice is constrained by laws of global economic relationships or some other immutable factor. It is a mindset that can influence how individual managers see their degree of choice, including decisions about whether to close a business. It is captured in the example

of a manager who worked 80–90 hours each week because he believed that there were simply not enough well qualified corporate lawyers to do his type of work. He expected to be caught in this situation indefinitely until the labour market changed. Rather than question his own role in this he saw the circumstances as outside his control.

A contrasting view of organisations is presented in the idea that they constantly adapt and change to different influences. In this 'living organism' mindset, it is the most adaptable organisations that are likely to survive. This is the home of the 'learning organisation' in which tacit and embedded organisational knowledge becomes the lifeblood of success. Arie de Geus captures this view in the best seller *The Living Company*. This ex-Shell executive compares the evolution of successful companies like the Sumitomo Corporation and the Swedish company Stora, to the evolution of birds and animals, which survive through timely adaptation to their environment.

This particular mindset has had considerable impact on the work of many training and development departments. A good example is to be found in Anglian Water, a UK private water company, where employees have been encouraged to embark on action learning projects known as 'transformational journeys'. In these projects the emphasis is not just on learning, but learning to learn, and then embedding those insights back into the organisation so that others can benefit. In this mindset each person makes a small difference to the organisation's adaptability, but the organisation has an independent life of its own.

There are other well-established mindsets that influence managerial thinking. For example, it is common to hear managers describing organisations in language borrowed from anthropologists. Their workplaces are mini-societies, organisational 'cultures' that then influence the way the inhabitants look at the world. From a very different view again organisations have sometimes been seen as oppressive instruments which dominate their employees, trapping and alienating them within soul-destroying jobs. Indeed, because organisations are many things at once there are a host of possible mindsets that

may influence management thinking, some more dominant and pervasive than others.

Having said that, such richness of imagery is not evident in every organisational circumstance. In fact what is most interesting about organisational mindsets from our point of view is the consistent appearance of two in particular – the rational corporate pyramid and the 'alternative' world of organisational politics.

Despite the increasing sophistication of organisational forms, the basic archetype of top-down authority structures – the rational economic model of organisations – still prevails. Implicit in the rational model is the need for top-down co-ordination, control and power. Strategy is aligned with structures and corporate values. Organisational problems are approached logically and analytically and these managerial attributes are essential if organisational goals are to be achieved efficiently and effectively. Over 500 years of successful commercial activity have been built on this pyramid model of organisation.

However, as many management theorists have pointed out, top level managers are coming to recognise the limitations of this classic model, particularly in terms of flexibility and speed of response in rapidly changing business environments. Yet although structures have flattened, tilted sideways towards matrix models, and employees have become more empowered, organisations still need some form of hierarchical control. Managers still need to determine direction, allocate resources and monitor performance and thus the hierarchical mindset remains very real.

The political mindset appears to dominate management thinking in equal measure but is more often than not a concept with deep negative connotations. One of the reasons for this is that the hierarchical model suppresses the inevitable partisan interests of organisational life. As we saw in Chapter 1, this conflict of interests is particularly evident in the arena of change management.

Cash Co. embarked on a culture change programme in the mid-1990s, attempting to move the company towards a greater market and customer led strategy. In the past it had a reputation for technical excellence, a strong product focus and an efficient command and control structure. The new strategy involved the creation of multidisciplinary teams focused on specific customers or groups of customers. These became the cornerstones of the new approach. Organisation values were aligned around a common set of principles that promoted respect for the individual and team working. Country directors had to become 'coaches', and to support their teams rather than manage them. They were expected to empower them with greater levels of autonomy and move 'from knowing all to learning continuously'. Yet for the most part, while the structure had changed, directive behaviour prevailed. For some established country managers the reorganisation had struck hard at their individual job motivation and identity, and it seemed to them to diminish the value that they brought to the organisation. So through a process of covert resistance they publicly accepted but privately rejected the new structure and within a year many elements of the new model were falling into disrepute. The advocates of the change programme saw these tactics as disingenuous and unprincipled.

Politics and rationality were surely the order of the day in Cash Co. On the face of it they are strange bedfellows, and in their purest forms, mutually exclusive. In the rational model there needs to be unity of purpose, common goals and interests to ensure efficiency. In the political mindset common goals are difficult to identify, and there will always be conflicting interests and

ambitions. Each mindset undermines the 'logic' of the other. As we will see later in this chapter, each contains different linguistic conventions and different patterns of motivation and incentives. Yet it is the clash of these two models that represents everyday experience for management.

Take the case of Bob. While he was away from the office on business for a week (or perhaps because he was away) his boss laid plans to reorganise substantially the credit function in which he worked, leaving him 'out in the cold'. Realising what had happened, Bob began a process of lobbying and alliance building to provide an alternative structure for the future of the department. In his plan he was able to demonstrate improved progress towards a key organisational goal. He succeeded in reversing the decision, and manoeuvred himself into a position where he was managing some of the peers who had supported his boss's plan. In one sense he was reinforcing the rational mindset by restructuring towards a common organisational goal, while at the same time subverting the same top-down model through the use of political action.

What then, are the implications for managers if their thinking is dominated by these two mindsets? There are three that are of special importance. First, as we noted previously, hierarchy is widely acknowledged to be a problematic mechanism of co-ordination and control in the contemporary business environment. Ironically, therefore, adherence to the rational mindset gets in the way of effective management. Second, the values embedded in hierarchical control tend to surround 'organisational politics' with strong negative connotations. As in the world of government, 'politicians' can have a somewhat disrep-

utable image. The result is that managers are caught between legitimacy and reality, a confusing and unwelcome dilemma to be faced with. Finally, and in consequence, the intrinsic value of a political frame of reference remains largely unrecognised as a valuable alternative means through which managers can achieve results. This has ever-increasing significance in the context of today's business environment.

These key implications are discussed in depth for the remainder of the chapter. In this way we hope to show the reader the difficulty of moving beyond the rational mindset, and the dramatic potential of embracing the political dimension of organisations.

Hierarchy and Top-down Control

In order to be able to respond quickly to rapidly changing market conditions, organisations need to be able to make decisions closer to customers. Hierarchical decision-making is too slow and cumbersome for these conditions. In the new economy enterprise, hierarchy is of course still an organising principle, but it is equally a fact of organisational life that business-critical knowledge is as likely to be held by front-line staff as by senior management. Richer Sounds, for example, a UK hi-fi retailer with one of the highest sales per square metre of any retailer in the world, recognises this by rewarding all staff suggestions regardless of their usefulness, and each employee submits around 20 suggestions a year.

Successful companies are those that are able to identify and leverage this tacit or taken-for-granted knowledge. It has necessitated substantial delayering, alignment around key processes, dramatic increases in horizontal co-ordination and team working, and the need to balance properly input from the corporate centre with local line autonomy. Management theorists argue that all this places a new requirement on managerial roles. Top level executives need to move from their traditional role of

resource allocation to become institutional leaders, creating and embedding a sense of organisational *raison d'être*. The role of senior managers also changes. They cease being administrative controllers and become supportive coaches of independent front-line business units. In turn the role of managers within business units changes from operational implementation to innovative entrepreneurship.

Businesses such as 3M, Asea Brown Boveri (ABB) and Virgin have long been trying to work according to these principles, and have become famous within the world of management for their approach to organising. But a wealth of detailed research within many organisations that have attempted to make these fundamental shifts suggests very patchy success. Put simply, they are very difficult to achieve. There is often little impact made on the hierarchical status quo, and that leaves managers particularly vulnerable. For instead of helping to create organisations that combine nimbleness with all the traditional virtues of scale and breadth, they find themselves caught in many paradoxes and double binds, becalmed in an ambiguous middle ground between corporate control and local opportunity. They can become 'damned if they do and damned if they don't', and end up pleasing nobody, as the case of Khalil shows.

Khalil found himself in this position when he was promoted to the position of Sales and Marketing Manager for a market sector in an electronics company. The division had not been performing well, morale was low, and there were a number of staff vacancies. On taking up his new appointment he found that he was required by head office to grow market share, while local management wanted to increase sales revenue. In the market for which he was responsible these two demands were almost mutually exclusive, and initially he felt he had been presented with 'mission impossible'.

After a great deal of agonising Khalil decided that the only way he could avoid being the 'meat in the sandwich' (as he called it) was by deft political manoeuvring. So he set out to explore the needs of each key stakeholder, and with the help of his team, was able to come up with a solution that met each party's requirements. But there was a large personal cost because resolving the conflicting demands took up a lot of Khalil's time, and he had to take a number of personal risks along the way.

It is a situation mirrored in many organisations. Khalil was prepared to work with covert political motives, but how many in his situation would have done the same? The persistent acceptance of the hierarchical imperative by many managers would have left them with no way out, unable to see the kind of solution that Khalil identified.

Even where you might least expect to find it, as, for instance, in knowledge intensive industries like consultancies or universities, the rational mindset is alive and well. For example the position of partner in many large consultancy firms is still considered to be the forum for most organisational decision-making, even though there is substantial pressure for knowledge-driven organisations to structure around empowerment and autonomy. Significantly, many writers in the field of knowledge management are still bemoaning the slow transformation of these types of organisation, rather than being able to hold them up as exemplars to the rest of the world. Empowerment remains very 'managerial'; control and authority are still the focus of attention rather than leadership and the exploitation of diverse interests.

Of course the pervasive nature of the rational mindset does not imply that each and every aspect of hierarchical management is problematic in the new economy. It is in the nature of

organisations to reflect an element of hierarchy. Different groups of people clearly have varying levels of contribution to make to their organisation, and it is self-evident that only certain individuals are able to make strategic contributions because most are necessarily engaged in short-term activities. More fundamentally, some high level co-ordination is essential if the potential value of any large-scale organisation is to be realised, and without question, big organisations will remain a feature of the global economic landscape. Hierarchy, therefore, is not going to disappear, and we are not advocating its elimination. What matters is its dysfunctional impact on managers and their effectiveness, even when they know it is a deeply flawed principle of organising.

The Illegitimacy of Politics

How does the rational mindset serve to undermine the value of a political frame of reference, creating for managers like Bob and Khalil the dilemma of whether to accept the reality of organisations when that reality is not legitimate? There are four factors in particular that combine to create negative perceptions of political behaviour, at times with overwhelming efficiency. These are the myth of corporate unity, the impact of human resource philosophy, the power of organisational language, and lastly, the ease with which in an organisational context we can delude ourselves about what is happening. Let us take a closer look at each to see how they can conspire against us in our efforts to manage organisations realistically.

The Myth of Corporate Unity

A major contributing influence on the perceived illegitimacy of political action is the ideal of corporate unity. This is an organisational fundamental from the perspective of a rational mindset.

It implies that organisations simply do not have a *raison d'être* if they do not have unity of purpose. Mission statements, vision and value creeds all serve to bind organisational members together, to draw the boundaries between them and the rest of the world. Unity of purpose creates alignment between strategy and action – it shapes the behaviours of people so that they work for the common good. It all seems logical enough. However, the dysfunctional consequence of this drive for unity lies in the implicit denial of either the existence, or the value, of alternative agendas in the same organisation.

Imagine the impact of a corporate briefing couched in the following terms:

> We understand that this company is a loose federation of competing interest groups through which we negotiate to move forward towards a common strategy, if we can come up with one. So if you don't like the look of what is being proposed feel free to challenge these ideas and offer some alternatives. Bear in mind that you may well get some opposition, so it will almost certainly be important to lobby the right people if you want to get heard. Your best bet is to create some alliances and coalitions to help you because we don't have a formal arbitration process for doing this.

The power of the drive for unity renders this hard to take seriously. Yet to many managers, the coming together of the interests of organisational opinion-makers through self-styled alliances and coalitions is exactly the way strategy is formulated. Indeed given the inevitable differences between powerful organisational factions and individuals, how else could it be devised? Yet obvious as this question may seem, how admissible would it be in most organisations?

The beguiling logic of the unity ideal is most apparent at the level of corporate goals. It is also the place where it is most exposed, particularly to the outside world. Does the ultimate rationale for unity of purpose in publicly owned companies lie in shareholder value and the maximisation of share price? It is a powerful idea, so much so that if you ask any employee in a

major US-based corporation what its current stock price is, they will almost certainly be able to tell you. The undeniable logic of a company's financial success focuses everyone's mind, but in doing so can subordinate other fundamental goals, such as the desire to behave in a socially responsible way with respect to employees, the environment, the community, or developing countries. These are not inevitably in opposition to the achievement of financial goals but in reality often are, especially when profits are thin. Such 'stakeholder claims' reveal the strong conflict of interests within an organisation, sometimes exposed through media coverage, and played out through internal political action which is to do with everything except unity of purpose. Yet while those differences cannot always be hidden, the drive for unity ensures that they can be denied, glossed over or given a positive spin. The 'seamless' top team presents a picture of harmony that may well be challenged from outside the business, but if you are a manager on the inside – well, that's different. It is not 'right' to blow the whistle on the myth of unity.

Human Resource Management Ethos

The unity ideal has been reflected in many initiatives that are associated with Human Resource Management (HRM). Many commentators have noted that the mission of HRM is itself often unclear, but broadly speaking HRM strives to shape organisations by creating empowered workers, trusting employment relationships, a unified culture, and greater workforce commitment, or as one cynical business guru puts it, a bunch of happy campers. These ideals are born of a strong people-centred tradition in which organisations are seen as places where people can develop themselves and realise their personal potential. It represents a set of values that places a strong emphasis on collaboration, teamwork and openness.

This may be a compelling mission in its own right, and one that is a natural adjunct to the notion of unity. It does not seek to ignore, so much as suppress the political realities of organ-

isations. However, there is an additional twist. The HRM mission does not sit easily alongside the immediacy of stock prices and shareholder value. Despite attempts to shift the outlook of the investment community to take a wider view of 'human capital', the power of the marketplace in a competitive global economy inevitably results in people being considered as extensions of capital assets. In times of downturn it is people, 'our greatest asset' who are downsized to preserve security for those remaining. Such actions naturally foster cynicism about organisational values emphasising the importance of employees, and HRM processes can become seen as subtle methods of control. Corporate unity is still the aim, but the method is (even) more insidious. Similarly induction programmes, psychometric tests to select and promote employees, and competency frameworks can come to be viewed as methods to enforce conformity in attitude and behaviour. The management theorist Hugh Willmott likens this to the double speak of Orwell's *1984*. Take the example of a manager who attended an in-house development programme designed to help him understand his business's new strategic direction. In his words, 'it was indoctrination; the implicit message was do things this way or get out'. In this instance the business lost an opportunity to engage a thinking manager in the strategy-making process, and the dysfunctional consequence of the drive for conformity was demotivation.

The discrediting of political differences through the mechanism of HRM values is particularly well illustrated in the move towards greater team working. As organisations seek to increase horizontal co-ordination in order to leverage cross-functional synergies, there has been a dramatic explosion in team development, and 'team player' is a key item in most competency frameworks. Encouraged by the HRM drive for collaborative working, management often holds embedded values about ideal teams that stress openness, trust and selfless motivation. Yet the diversity of individual motives in organisations has always made genuine teamwork extremely hard to achieve, so why should that have changed? Quite aside from the improbable notion of selfless motivation, there are many reasons why indiv-

idual and partisan organisational agendas take precedence over the high ideals of unitary goals. Yet managers are continually encouraged to lead high performing teams and to be team players themselves. Unsurprisingly, when they perceive they have been 'let down' by others pursuing different agendas and priorities, it tends to confirm the view that self-interest is illegitimate. It is anti-team.

In one charity we know, this HRM drive for team working has become so strong that it is a fundamental principle in the organisation that no one should even discuss his or her individual interests. This commitment to the charitable cause is supposed to be total. On the surface, at least, all self-interest is denied. One of the charity's senior managers, Marie-Claire, was keen to reposition the work of her internal service function to add more value to the organisation. In doing so she needed to challenge a significant number of unspoken organisational practices, but for some time was frustrated at her lack of progress. She found herself coming up against many dead ends. Following a discussion with an external executive coach she recognised that she had not taken account of the real interests of those to whom she had been talking. But faced with the complete refusal to acknowledge self-interest, how could she do so? Encouraged by her coach, Marie-Claire listened much harder to what her colleagues said – not the actual words used, but the meanings behind them – and found that she was able to discuss their individual interests 'in code', as she described it. In the end she succeeded in implementing her plan and as a result worked herself into a position where she was chairing an influential committee on the future of the charity.

This is not to say that conformity and collaboration have no value in themselves. Of course sometimes they do. But the over-riding dominance of the HRM message, as Marie-Claire discovered, undermines the constructive value of politics, conflict, dissension and self-interest as worthwhile in organisational terms. The HRM push for alignment of values and behaviours can imply that anything other than complete commitment to, and identification with, organisational goals is problematic.

The Power of Language

The third factor which influences the perceived illegitimacy of political action is the way language is used to promote unity of organisational purpose. Language, of course, is a fundamental part of the process through which we create the organisational mindsets, and through well-crafted communication, managers are able to influence employee perceptions that lead to the acceptance of one meaning rather than another. An interesting example is provided by management researchers who have studied the images that senior management use in writing annual reports. Implicit in these were assumptions of corporate unity; employees being described as working hard for the company, loyal and dedicated to it, and overcoming challenges faced by the entire organisation in difficult business circumstances.

The power of language to define our perceptions is no more evident than in the language of organisational change. It can be found embedded in all types of corporate briefings, induction and education processes, as well as change management seminars. Words carry implicit meanings beyond their face value and can provide a rich subtext of additional understanding for the recipient. Working from within a rational mindset, words have the effect of creating a sense of logic, order and structure, reinforcing the notion that change can be planned, directed and, most important of all, driven through the hierarchy.

Take, for example, words and phrases such as:

- business case
- top-down
- staged transformation
- cascading the vision
- corporate initiative
- smooth transition
- strategic intent
- facilitated process
- planned modification

These are frequently found in the organisational communications that explain and support change initiatives. Used in this context they tend to imply direction, control, certainty and rationality. These implicit messages reinforce the idea that change can be managed on the basis of top-down control.

The HRM message of trust and collaboration also has a high profile in the language of change. Consider the following:

- empowerment
- co-operation
- core values
- openness
- development
- cross-collaboration
- trust
- teamwork
- unlocking potential

These are also frequently associated with change management. But in contrast they imply a positive, humanistic enlightened perspective, that change is liberating and beneficial for employees. Taken together these ideas of enlightenment and control provide a compelling rationale for change that further legitimates the hierarchical mindset from which it is derived.

Not surprisingly, against the force of this language it is difficult for managers to entertain thoughts of open

dissension and confrontation on anything other than minor issues. The language of political activity appears to question motives, to ask why, to challenge. Words that describe political activity have thus been attributed negative meanings, even if the motives behind them are intended to be in the best long-term interests of the organisation. Contrast the words and phrases below with those just considered:

- stealth
- covert action
- positioning
- degrading the status quo
- personal networking
- irreverence
- lobbying
- corridor talk
- power base

All of these have come to embody the illegitimacy of political processes. The inference is that the subversion of organisational objectives does not constitute appropriate managerial action.

Few managers wish to curtail good quality debate about important organisation issues, but the language of rational management can be sufficiently powerful for that to be the effect. Potential challenge can become driven underground and transformed into the language of subversion, thereby reinforcing the organisational unacceptability of political behaviour. So strong is this definition of illegitimacy in some managerial contexts, that one very senior member of an international financial services organisation we know attempts to censor the language of those around him. He refuses to have the 'P' word uttered in his presence, and not surprisingly, his more junior colleagues comply.

Self-delusion and the Moral High Ground

Many social commentators have noted that organisations play a significant role in defining an individual manager's self-identity. Moreover, as other arenas that help secure stable identities in our wider society decay, such as the church and community, the self-identity derived from jobs and work increases. At the same time, it is only human to be selective when interpreting feedback about our own work performance in an effort to protect our feelings of self-worth. Unfortunately, this complex set of factors creates the circumstances in which we may delude ourselves about the political nature of organisations in order to preserve our own identity. Let us take the example of managerial career advancement to show how this can happen.

From within the rational mindset, organisations are implicit meritocracies in which we progress as a direct consequence of effective personal contribution. This in turn assumes others (in particular the boss) to be working objectively on our behalf to ensure that this contribution gets due organisational recognition. So when we are passed over for promotion how do we deal with these 'injustices' of managerial decision-making? To accept non-rational explanations of organisational career planning processes would require an appreciation of their political nature. This is potentially destabilising if you are committed to organisational rationality, and it is understandable that some managers insist on maintaining an apolitical interpretation of the circumstances surrounding them. In fact, so great is the psychological security derived from implicit rational values, that researchers have shown managers to be capable of engaging in apparently co-operative work practices, while unaware that they are ignoring their own (obvious) efforts to profit at the expense of others.

In the same way managers are able to construe negative politics as something that is done to them and not something they do to others. Consider Philip, a manager on a business school development programme. With obvious disdain in his voice, he explained that he did not get involved in politics, and refused to have anything to do with those in his business who were polit-

ical. He did not allow them to interact with his team and he gave them no more information than he had to. As he spoke, his fellow participants broke into smiles, quickly to be replaced by open amusement, as they quickly saw his views and actions were inherently political. Philip, it seemed, was the one person in the room unaware of the implications of what he was saying. As his colleagues explained to him later, in taking the moral high ground he had set out to exempt himself from the unacceptability of organisational politics, but had succeeded in doing so only in his own eyes.

The Combined Effect

The reader can probably see by now the potency of the combined effect of this drive for unity, the HRM ethos, the reinforcing role of language, and the very human need to protect the self-image. Together these conditions create a circularity of thinking that is difficult to penetrate, or even to question. In consequence it can be difficult to see the potential value of the alternative mindset – that of constructive politics (see Figure 2.1).

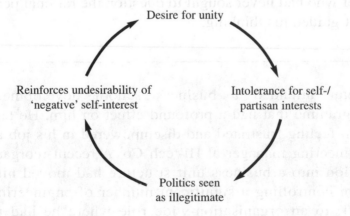

Figure 2.1 The circularity of the rational mindset

But the dubious virtuosity of this circle can be broken. Far from frustrating organisation activity, the political perspective can create greater autonomy and freedom for managers and greater organisational effectiveness than strict adherence to rationality ever could. However, as we have tried to show, this constructive interpretation of organisational politics is often lost to managers. It is this that we now turn to, for it is the third of the fundamental implications we identified that follow from the dominance of the rational and political mindsets.

The Unrealised Value of Politics

Our analysis leads to the natural conclusion that the potential value of a political mindset is still to be actualised in many organisations. Yet political activity defined as constructive is more than achievable. It is very different to its negative counterpart in several fundamental ways, as we will set out to explain in the next chapter. Compared with the obvious manoeuvring driven by pure self-interest, constructive political activity is far more skilful. To begin to see why, let us take an in-depth look at how real political fluency was achieved by a manager who had never sought to question the rational perspective that guided his thinking.

Dieter attended a business school development programme that had a profound effect on him. He had been feeling frustrated and disempowered in his job as engineering manager at Hi-tech Co. A recent reorganisation into a business unit structure had moved him from controlling a significant number of engineering staff, to an organisation-wide role where he had to achieve results through personal influence rather than

by direct authority. According to his sponsor for the programme, 'Dieter had encountered significant resistance to his efforts to push forward on site', and it was hoped that the programme 'would challenge Dieter and give him some understanding of the game'. An interesting choice of language, you might think, for a sponsor of executive development.

As a result of the programme two key learning points emerged. First, Dieter's own style needed to change if he was to be able to exert greater influence in the plant. He himself described this style as 'I'm right', 'insensitive to others' and 'argumentative'. Second, he saw that if he were going to restructure the engineering role at Hi-tech Co, he would have to accept and work with the very different agendas of the key business unit leaders (BULs), rather than arguing through the logic of his own viewpoint.

On returning to work Dieter set about managing his influence with much greater political fluency. He dealt with the BULs as individuals, asking questions around their agendas and business drivers. He established himself on several influential committees with the specific intention of building key relationships, and in order to have a forum for making presentations on engineering value and business benefit. He benchmarked the performance of the engineering function, both internally and externally with competitors, and collected customer satisfaction data as evidence that the current approach could be improved. Using this to propose some changes, he then worked with the different agendas and varying levels of acceptance and resistance among the BULs, eventually obtaining agreement for one business unit to act as a prototype for his new arrangements. This in turn allowed him to embark on a much broader assessment of

required engineering competencies, which generated further data to support his reorganisation of the engineering function, as well as improve training and resourcing activities. Approximately a year after his development programme Dieter was given the go ahead to implement his ideas.

Reflecting on his progress at that point Dieter was struck by several key insights which really underline why a political perspective can be so positive in achieving results:

- First, he was able to make things happen himself without relying on formal authority. However, this meant he had to invest considerable amounts of his time in managing upwards and sideways. In effect Dieter had come to de-emphasise the significance of hierarchy and superior–subordinate relationships because he realised how much he could influence these.

- He was able to see how it was possible to influence more of the future for himself and was able to engage in organisational relationships with less concern for his own security. As he saw it, things were more likely to change if he took responsibility for influencing that change. His experience had provided him with greater feelings of personal control and self-satisfaction.

- He recognised that the competing agendas he had encountered among the BULs actually presented opportunities to achieve what he believed was right for the organisation, and for him. Having recognised the inevitability of these competing interests he had been able to harness the different perspectives to challenge the status quo.

From the outset Dieter had seen what was required from a rational business perspective. But for him to bring this about, a challenge to his own organisational mindset had been necessary. In effect Dieter had been able to take a more critical perspective of what was happening around him in Hi-tech Co. By adopting a positive approach to the inevitability of politics, he had the confidence to work in, what was for him, a very novel way. Most importantly, he could see that he had a choice. In the words of the management theorist Nick Perry:[1]

What defines the idea of politics is the conviction that there is always an alternative; its voluntaristic premise is that social life can be other than it is. The clash of interests, opinion, debate and compromise is the very stuff of political practice.

In accomplishing this shift of mindset, Dieter implicitly recognised that political activity is open to many different interpretations according to different situations. This realisation had required him to avoid negative interpretations of his actions by being open about his agenda of improving organisational effectiveness. He had appreciated the influence of the rational mindset on the BULs by producing logical evidence and hard data to support his views, and piloted his solution in good project management fashion. Yet while doing this he had been lobbying key stakeholders and surfacing unspoken agendas.

All that said, it is not our intention to suggest that a constructive political perspective should triumph conclusively over rational management, or that it is, in itself, unproblematic. We cannot dispense with hierarchy, and while the political mindset realises the possibility and relevance of individual power in achieving results, there is a real question as to how this power should be used in the interests of an organisation, without it being diverted substantially towards self-serving ends. In the rational mindset power is congruent with authority and seniority of position, and in theory, is not abused. In practice, of course, it is, but in emphasising the importance of individual self-determination, there is a risk that we swap one contentious use of power for

48 *Smart Management*

another. Furthermore, power is not evenly distributed and organisations are not level playing fields. Power is invested to differing degrees in different roles, and no amount of self-determination or recognition of competing interests will completely remove the inequalities of organisational power distribution. It is to the nature of power that we now turn in the next chapter, its principled use, and the balance that is necessary for any manager to strike between organisational and self-interest.

1. Perry, Nick (1998) *Organisation Studies*, Spring, **19**(2), 235

CHAPTER 3

Legitimate Politics

There is no opting out. Like it or not, politics play a central role in all organisations. Being a politician is part of the job for management. Our key objective now is to help the reader to appreciate the logic of constructive organisational politics, since without that starting point, no manager is likely to be motivated to enhance his or her own political skill. Emancipation from the myth of rationality is the goal, but that is much more difficult to achieve so long as politics are seen as illegitimate or, at best, a necessary organisational evil. Seasoned managers are often ambivalent towards politics once they accept that so many organisational decisions are driven by partisan interest, and that the idea of a meritocracy is more of an ideal than a reality. But ambivalence is no recipe for crystal-clear thinking, and will always be insufficient to generate an appetite for true political competence. Nothing short of a constructive political mindset will suffice. However, we can hardly expect you, the reader, to reach beyond the intellectual curiosity that has allowed us to keep your attention so far without offering a watertight rationale for thinking of politics as legitimate organisational activity. With this in mind, we will look in this chapter at the way in which power is thought about and used in organisations, and how this relates to the motivations of managers. The reason for this is that

motives are the only final way of distinguishing legitimate politics from their less acceptable counterpart.

We define politics as those deliberate efforts made by individuals and groups in organisations to use power in pursuit of their own particular interests. It must follow that whatever is seen as an acceptable interest will give us some strong clues about how to develop the idea of legitimate politics. We will begin by asking the question 'What is meant by power?' It is crucial to provide a clear answer to this because, despite the obvious use of organisational power that all managers witness day by day, it is an elusive concept. We will then try to thread a course through the difficult problems of the use and misuse of power, and of means that do not justify ends. In the process of this we will draw parallels with the principles of democratic political systems to help create the logic for legitimising organisational politics. One notable similarity we will consider is how many of the vexed issues surrounding organisational politics seem to be a microcosm of the difficulties people see in upholding the principles of democratic government. In contrast, however, while many managers may struggle with the idea of legitimising organisational politics, few argue that the principles of political democracy should be abandoned. We will try to show the reader that there is much to be gained from transferring some of the cherished principles of democratic government to organisational settings and that failure to do so represents flawed thinking, which only makes the task of managing more difficult.

The Problem of Power

We describe power as problematic for two reasons. First, as so many of the management and organisational thinkers to study the subject have found, it is difficult to define organisational power. This is surprising in some respects because on the face of it, there often appears to be little doubt about who is

powerful and why they are able to wield their power. However, on closer inspection, there is complexity and contradiction surrounding the concept of organisational power, which in reality has a direct impact on any attempt to use it in the management process. Second, the potential and actual use of power raises moral dilemmas for managers that are a source of confusion, and in some circumstances, deep anxiety. Power draws our attention to the issues of personal responsibility that lie at the heart of management, and to the question of how much individual executives should contribute to the organisations that employ them. We will set out to unravel the problematic face of power in the discussion that follows.

The Definition of Power

The definition of power commonly used by organisation theorists is straightforward enough, and rarely quarrelled over. Power is described as the capacity of individuals and groups to impress their own preferences upon others, to exert their will in such a way that those people do things they might not otherwise do. So far so good. But like most universal definitions, this glosses over a number of important distinctions and conceptual puzzles that have a bearing on the clarity of our analysis. In particular there are three questions that require our attention in order to grasp the essential characteristics of power:

- First, how much is power really a capacity that can be attributed to specific individuals or groups? Is it a possession, in other words?

- Second, does power have to be perceived in order that we can say it is being exercised?

- Third, how central to any organisational process is power, or to put it differently, when do we *not* exercise power over one another?

We will address each of these questions in turn. However, the aim is not to provide final answers. That is not possible anyway since the questions represent the different aspects of power that make it the complex phenomenon we know it to be. Our aim is to draw attention to the dangers of oversimplifying the idea of power, and so to the importance of recognising from a managerial point of view what is actually happening in the exercise of power.

Is Power a Specific Capacity of Particular People or Groups?

The idea of power being possessed by a particular person or group is very seductive. It accords with common sense and is our everyday experience of organisations. When we say that certain people have more 'organisational clout' or 'stripes' than others do, we simply mean that as individuals, they have greater power to get things moving, or to arrest them. Much the same is meant when a particular person is described as 'very persuasive'. We are impressed by their ability to put together an argument, the breadth and depth of their intellect, their enthusiasm or their natural charm. What lies behind this view of somebody is the idea of he or she *owning* something that enables them to influence us if they choose to do so. In the above examples there is in fact an important distinction between what are known as 'situational' sources of power (for example, hierarchical position), and 'personal' sources (such as personality traits). Both appear to be thought of and talked about as though they are directly attached to certain individuals and groups. We will examine each more closely before answering our question.

Management and organisation theorists have studied these sources of power in depth and as a result much is now known about them. There are several types to be found in both the situational and personal categories.

Primary situational sources of power include:

■ *Formal authority which stems from hierarchy.* Traditionally known as 'legitimate power' it derives its lawful status from

the core social value of rational economic organisation, in which the tasks of control and co-ordination intrinsically create a pyramid structure. Sociologists have shown how this value has come to assume great significance for twentieth-century society, fundamentally determining the 'natural' shape of organisations in the process. Hierarchical position, or as it is often known, 'position power', is directly associated with 'the right to manage', and as we described in the previous chapter, expectations of conformity appear to be a deeply embedded mindset. We should note, however, that this very same authority structure also gives position power to people at non-managerial levels in the hierarchy. Sometimes referred to as 'gatekeepers', those occupying certain lower echelon roles can impede managerial initiatives by pointing out that they are being asked to do something which is not their job, or which runs contrary to the rules. The right to 'play it by the book' can be used to counter the right to manage even though as power bases they are of the same rootstock – rational organisation.

■ *Control over the flow of information.* This is the old idea that 'information is power'. Despite the liberating effects of information technology, it appears to be alive and well for the simple reason that there are always good organisational reasons to manage information flow. 'Classified information' is not just a formal way of recognising restricted access: it refers just as much to what people unofficially choose to withhold from others. People 'in the know' have a tendency to 'privatise' information, especially when they have gone out of their way to acquire it. It is also well known that groups and individuals at the corporate centre tend to be powerful because of their proximity to key information sources. Physical closeness can be an important factor even in today's world where 'geography does not matter'.

■ *The significance of an individual or group to the organisation.* It is said that 'nobody is indispensable' but in practice they may be, at least in the short term, because others are dependent on

them. Theorists have studied the dependencies between the range of key areas of activity within organisations and found that when one unit is in a position to reduce uncertainty for others, it enjoys a powerful position. A universally recognised example is the role played by finance functions that, in controlling spend, influence certainty of work for other parts of an organisation. There is always relief when the budget is approved. Significance, not surprisingly, is frequently associated with the ability to control 'hard' resource – money and headcount.

■ *Control over 'hard' rewards.* Career progression, remuneration, continued employment and autonomy of operation are all obvious tangible rewards, and those who decide the fortunes of others are naturally seen as powerful individuals. Rewards must be valued by the beneficiaries if they are to function in this way, and we know from motivation theory that there are no universals in this respect. The reader may be wondering at this point why we have excluded the less tangible rewards of praise and recognition. It is because these are so closely bound up with the credibility of the person giving them that it is more useful to think of such person-specific factors as personal sources of power. We will refer to them again later in this discussion.

It is important to recognise that these situational sources of power are clearly distinct from one another. In other words, while one source may provide managers with access to another (for example, the authority which comes with position may imply control over hard rewards), those sources are nonetheless independent. So, for instance, although senior executives can usually wield a degree of authority within their own organisational patch, they may have limited access to critical information outside of that area. Whether or not they have inside track to key organisational decision-making processes may determine their ability to influence their own staff more than the authority of office. It must follow that when one person enjoys access to all

of the main sources of situational power there is real scope for organisational influence.

Situational sources of power are specific capacities of individuals to influence in the sense that those sources are awarded, gifted or acquired, and so are temporarily 'owned'. Personal sources of power, by contrast, are readily recognisable as individual capabilities. They are much more obviously permanent personal possessions. This appears to hold true the more these capacities to influence are thought of as personality traits of individuals. Since there are many personal attributes that may give their owners a special ability to influence others, there have been numerous attempts to classify them. These are the main categories:

■ *Referent power.* This is the ability to influence based on what others see as desirable personality traits. These personal dispositions are a point of reference for others; they provide the content for role modelling. Examples include integrity, emotional intelligence, ambition, drive, confidence and resilience. Leadership, it is often said, embodies these very qualities, and the true source of the leader's power is admiration. Personal attributes of this nature have a very strong association with inner psychological structure and are often taken to be innate to the individual. However, as with all personality traits, it is observed behaviour that provides the reference point for others. The traits themselves must be inferred. Since desirable behaviour can be copied, this opens the way for us to think of traits as qualities that can be learnt.

■ *Expertise.* When we believe that someone has knowledge and skills that are superior to our own, and we are willing to let them guide us, they exercise expert power. In organisational contexts this source of personal power is often associated with professional and highly specialised work, and those who possess expertise have often invested time and energy in acquiring it. Two features in particular of an expert body of knowledge determine its potency. To be usable it has to be

both credible and inaccessible to those the expert wishes to influence. Specialist managers and consultants, for example, are often unable to make their point stick because one of those conditions has not been met. Frequently it is a credibility problem. To compound matters, because expert knowledge is so strongly identified with individuals, other people may make no separation between the knowledge and the person. It is personal credibility that is at stake.

■ *Social competence.* There is little doubt that skills such as the ability to read the motives of others, present ideas engagingly, diffuse conflict, conduct interviews, behave in a collaborative fashion, or be good at small talk, are an important means of influencing. These are not expert skills and possessing them does not depend on knowing something that most other people do not (although it might feel like that when we are in situations where we feel least at ease). Take the example of giving praise or recognition to someone – the 'soft' rewards. Anybody can give recognition. You do not have to be a manager to commend the efforts of others, so it is not the same as being in the position to use the power of 'hard' reward. But to praise effectively it is necessary to sound sincere, to time it well, be specific, deal with negative reactions like disbelief or embarrassment, and to be sure not to overuse it. Once learnt, the skill of giving praise becomes a very personal source of power. The spotlight is not only on the recipient. It is on you too – it is *you* giving praise. But like most social skills it is difficult to learn and so may be in short supply. That is part of the power that comes with skill. Socially skilful managers compare favourably with their less able colleagues.

■ *Success.* We say that 'everyone loves a winner', that 'success breeds success'. But behind the clichés is more than a germ of truth. The value society puts on success ensures that the successful are powerful. Success denotes achievement, prosperity, victory, and social acceptance. It is associated with results, and to coin another phrase, you can't argue with those. Usually we attribute it to the efforts of particular indiv-

iduals and groups rather than explain it as the product of collective effort, the result of contributions too intertwined to unravel. Even when success is the result of good fortune we sometimes contrive to personalise it. Some people are lucky just as some are losers, we say. Broadly, though, the more success appears to be a direct consequence of deliberate effort the more it will be a source of personal power. Initiative takers know this well – success with one venture lends credibility to the next.

As with the situational sources of power discussed earlier, it is important to think of personal sources as being independent of one another, even though there may be obvious connections between them. Social competence, for instance, may seem to follow naturally from being a role model, but this is not necessarily the case. Personality may shine through in well-meant behaviour despite a lack of social skills. People often make allowances for the social ineptness of their leaders because they identify with their underlying personal qualities. But we recognise those qualities because of the way leaders behave, in other words, because of 'surface indicators'. Social skills, too, are evident primarily in behaviour, but behaviour that has often been systematically practised with the aim of producing 'managed performance'. Quite simply, not all behaviour is skilful but it may nevertheless be influential. Look at it the other way around. Social skill may prevent us from seeing the self-centred or even malign intentions of others because we are drawn by the plausibility of what they say and the way they say it.

In the preceding discussion we have described the primary sources of situational and personal power that appear to enable individuals and groups to influence others. Previously we had asked the question 'Is power a specific capacity of particular people or groups?' In other words, are we influenced by others because they are somehow personally in possession of the means to do so? At first glance the answer seems so obvious that the question should be dismissed as trivial. But as we will now show, on closer inspection there are some significant complica-

tions and exceptions to the extent that a simple answer is no longer possible.

It is true of course to say that a person can accumulate one or more sources of power. We can also say that several sources may be used to supplement one another, so that referent power may be used in parallel with position power, expert power with the power of social competence, and so on. But even where one person is able to bring several sources of power to bear, the scope to influence is restricted by circumstances, in particular the constraints imposed by the power base of other people, the domain of usability, and whether the power bases are perceived positively or negatively. We will look at each of these limits.

The old aphorism about the corrupting nature of absolute power lures us towards an essentially false premise. Power is not absolute. It is relative to that of others, unevenly distributed certainly, but never to the extent that there is no available counter influence process. Take expert power. Expertise can be disarmed or discredited through skilful challenge, marginalised by the success of organisational DIY, removed by authority, or met with yet more expertise. Authority is an even more revealing example. In the delayered and decentralised context of contemporary organisations it can be countered by every other source of power, which is of course why a greater understanding of politics is so important. Most sources of power can be challenged 'in kind'. Authority can be disputed by authority, success may be eclipsed by success. Control over information flow works both ways. Corporate centres, for example, need information from geographically distant operating units, which themselves scan the horizon for the early warning signals of impending organisational change. In both directions information is normally filtered and sometimes suspiciously sanitised. The underlying point here is that, although power is a capacity of individuals and groups, that capacity cannot in reality be used in isolation from the same capacity in others. It is particularly unwise to suppose power to be a capacity of particular people if 'particular' means 'only a few'. It is more useful to think of power as so widely distributed that it becomes a matter of practical enquiry as to who can influence whom.

Usable power is also confined to certain domains of application. Authority is appropriate only when the right to manage is recognised, expertise gains acceptance only where it is valued, success can be used to influence only where there is a common measure of achievement, and so on. This appears to be true even of referent power. Role modelling operates best within a limited sphere of established interpersonal relationships, which is why one of the tough decisions for senior executives is the judgement of how much time to devote to 'walking the talk' in their organisation. Mere reputation as visionary leader may promote curiosity but not often attraction. In fact reputation may work against the power of role modelling because when there is a lot to live up to shortcomings are amplified. Power may also be unusable in practice in situations because of convention. Pulling rank in public, offering rewards as bribes, being indiscreet with information, relying on the ignorance of others to impress with expertise (using technical jargon being a good example), are illustrations of how to transgress the rules about the responsible exercise of power. Perceptions, in other words, can intervene heavily. In addition, although sources of power are independent they do interact. Managers who have become role models, for instance, may find it difficult to use position power because others see it as unnecessary or inappropriate. Using authority diminishes the relationship. In effect the domain of position power is reduced, sometimes to the extent of becoming merely symbolic.

A further limit to the application of power is the tendency of those being influenced to perceive each power base positively or negatively according to its social acceptability. In other words, the different power bases vary in social worth. That can have the effect of reducing the scope to use certain of them in practice. So, for instance, while the exercise of 'hard' reward power is usually perceived as positive, the actual or suspected withholding of information gets a poor reception. Indispensability enjoys mixed fortunes in this respect, and the worth of expert power also often appears to hang in the balance. Attitudes towards authority, it is often said, have shifted markedly in a

negative direction during the latter part of the twentieth century. By contrast in the same period, the virtues of referent power have been increasingly extolled as leadership has climbed the organisational agenda. Broad as these social evaluations are, they impact on the ability of individuals to exercise power. It is further demonstration of the need for caution in assuming power to be unequivocally a direct possession of certain individuals that enables them to influence others.

Does Power Need To Be Perceived To Be Exercised?

In the preceding discussion we considered how power is problematic if we give simple answers to the question of who in organisations has it, and who does not. We now look at a second issue that needs unravelling in order to define power in a way which reflects practical reality for managers. This is the question of how much the perceptions of those involved play an active part in the exercise of power. Does it make sense to say that we can influence others without realising it, or that we can be influenced to do things we might not otherwise do without knowing what is happening? The answer is yes, but only if we accept that 'potential' awareness is sufficient for our definition of power. If I inadvertently discover I am being influenced, for example, or it is pointed out to me, then I can choose whether or not I continue to comply. I might also be unaware of the extent of my power until I witness its effects. It is therefore a question that alerts us to the possibility of power in organisations existing and being applied without the awareness of either the user or the target of influence. Power is used literally in ignorance. In the context of an organisational mindset that seeks to redefine politics as legitimate, this possibility has great significance. Ignorance may be bliss but it is no recipe for political competence.

Clearly there are many situations in which all concerned know that power is being exercised, and our earlier discussion highlighted the role of perception in moderating its application. However, there are some exceptions to this, which lead to the

compelling conclusion that power is independent of awareness. That is why the caveat of 'potential' awareness is necessary.

One such exception stems from what is known as the 'embedded' nature of power, the shorthand used by the theorists to describe hidden properties of situational sources of influence. Authority is a good example. When the power embedded in organisational structures is sufficiently accepted as the natural order of things, then awareness is dimmed and people may react less than knowingly. Not only are people influenced without their awareness, but those wielding the power do so without realising it (rather like 'not knowing your own strength'). Take the case of a manager who wants to generate some new ideas about how to solve a long running issue. She may say to one of her team something like: 'Maybe we should have a fresh look at the problem. Have you thought of trying this?' The next thing she knows is that 'this' has been put in place. Her effort to generate some creative thinking has been interpreted as a direct request for action. Neither she nor her team member has fully understood the taken-for-granted nature of her position power, which in effect appears to have been exercised unintentionally. She set out to downplay the relevance of authority to the situation, preferring to adopt a coaching style. In contrast, her team member has unquestioningly assumed that the right to give a directive has been exercised. The manager may then set out to repair the situation by questioning how this happened. However, it is only once authority has been questioned retrospectively (in theory by either party) that the embeddedness is revealed and awareness restored. It follows that either person in our example may become aware of the embedded power of the situation and choose not to reveal this to the other. In that circumstance the 'innocent' party is more open still to influence without their knowledge.

This example reveals the process through which power can be employed without the awareness of either party being necessary, and in principle these circumstances may arise in relation to each situational source of power described earlier. The control over information flow and hard rewards may therefore become so

assumed that it is unwittingly exercised and unquestioningly accepted. But the idea of embeddedness can also apply to personal sources of power. Referent power, or social competence, for instance, can become so taken for granted that, in effect, they go unnoticed in relationships. Sometimes people do not appreciate the force of their own personalities, and from a vantage point external to a relationship, those they influence may appear to be held spellbound by strength of character, easily swayed by silver-tongued manipulation. The awareness of 'outsiders', in other words, can be greater than that of 'insiders' who are immersed in a relationship. This is a key point because it again draws our attention to the idea that only potential awareness is necessary for power to be exercised.

Power is also deliberately concealed in organisations so that it can be exercised without the knowledge of the target of influence. Conversations take place behind closed office doors, on journeys, over a drink – anywhere that makes transparency impossible. Inaccessible committees, for example, settle budgeting and resource levels, withhold promotions and bonuses, and block career opportunities. The people they are making decisions about may never know just how much they have gained or lost. In addition, the decision-makers may successfully introduce hidden personal agendas by skilful manipulation of these discussions. We are often told, for instance, of meetings in which senior managers present well reasoned arguments for not promoting a rising managerial star on the basis that he or she 'is not ready for it yet'. The outcome is a 'rational' decision not to promote, but those who took part are left with the suspicion that the real agenda was age, sex or ethnic discrimination, personal threat, or vindictiveness. In circumstances like these the power being wielded is obscured by the private nature of both the discussion and the motives. However, this opaqueness in no way lessens its impact – quite the reverse since there is no means of mounting any challenge. In our example it is clear that the ultimate target – the fast track executive – has been influenced without his or her perception of power being applied.

When Do We Not Exercise Power?

The third question which helps us to understand the nature of power focuses on the kind of managerial actions that should be associated with the use of power, and those which should not. This question arises because it is possible to define almost any social interaction as an influence process, and hence any behaviour as an attempt to exercise power. However, this is not helpful since ultimately it makes the concept of power redundant. Nevertheless, there is some clarification necessary.

Even the most ordinary circumstances encountered in the daily routines of organisations can be seen as complex situations of potential and actual influence processes. Suppose, for instance, you are scheduled to make a presentation in a management meeting today. What decisions will you have already taken? Several regarding the presentation content, format and delivery style. Some further ones about how to answer certain questions. Perhaps more still about what to wear, when to arrive, or how much to engage in conversation with anyone beforehand. As you move through the presentation itself you will have to adjust to your audience's reactions. Should you answer a certain question now, later or ignore it altogether? How about revealing more on a particular point than you had planned, shortening what you intend to say, or lightening the atmosphere with some humour? And how should you respond to reactions after you leave the meeting? Play things down, open up a further discussion, challenge an implied criticism, ensure that everyone knows it went well? There will be layers of questions, all of which could be said to represent opportunities for you to enhance or exercise your power in the role of presenter. Irrespective of whether your power comes from authority, expertise, social competence or any other of the various situational and personal sources discussed earlier, we are left puzzling over where the use of that power begins and ends.

The theorists are divided about this. At one extreme there are those who argue that we are caught up in pervasive power struc-

tures which influence and shape our thinking and behaviour, even in the most mundane aspects of our lives. All social interaction potentially involves the exercise of power. At the other end of the spectrum power is seen as just one of many ways of understanding relationships and social processes. Co-operation, trust, exchange and selflessness (such as serving a worthy cause) are examples of concepts that have been extensively employed by social theorists from a range of disciplines to grasp the nature of society. Power, therefore, may be irrelevant as a way of explaining behaviour in many circumstances.

Evidently there is no simple answer to the question of what makes the exercise of power a distinctive process. The divergent positions just mentioned arise to some extent because theorists have very different agendas with regard to the constitution of the social world in the first place, which leads them to very different conclusions. However, many take the view that power is exercised on what is known as an 'episodic' basis, which means that it is observable in particular situations, at particular points in time, being deployed by certain individuals. This does not preclude circumstances where the use of power escapes detection, since as we have already noted, so long as it can potentially be perceived, we can say it is being exercised.

The value of thinking about the exercise of power in episodic terms, then, lies in being able to pinpoint circumstances where this occurs, and to distinguish power usage from other kinds of social processes that arise in organisations. There is direct significance in this from a managerial point of view. The ability to recognise where opportunities exist to use power is a very practical capability. On the other hand, associating each and every aspect of organisational life with power can lead to unnecessary expenditure of energy, or worse, destructive scepticism, even paranoia. Processes such as building trust and co-operation become even more troublesome than they already are because it is difficult to see them as worthy motives in their own right. Being able to identify the difference between the exercise of power as a key feature of certain organisational processes, and power as the defining characteristic of all

processes, is, therefore, a key managerial competence. This brings us again to a point we have already sought to emphasise strongly in this chapter. Awareness is an essential to effective use of power for managers.

Power: A Summary

Situational Sources of Power

- Formal authority: the 'legitimate power' derived from managerial positions.

- Control of information: leveraging access and dissemination of formal or informal information.

- Significance of individuals or groups to an organisation: the ability to reduce uncertainty for others.

- Control over hard rewards: rewards valued by the beneficiary, for example career progression, remuneration and so on.

Personal Sources of Power

- Referent (leadership/role model): personality traits that provide observed behaviour that is seen as desirable by others, for example integrity, confidence, resilience and so on.

- Expertise: knowledge which is both credible yet inaccessible to those being influenced.

- Social competence: high order social skills such as reading others' motives, diffusing conflict and so on.

> ■ Success: the influence that comes with achievement, victory and so on that appears to be a direct consequence of deliberate effort.

Politics as the Application of Power

The aim of the preceding discussion was to answer the question 'What is power?' We stressed the need to recognise that, although it appears self-evident that certain individuals possess power, there are several situational and personal sources, and each has a limited domain of application. We then considered how it is often possible in organisations for power to be exercised without the awareness of those being influenced. Finally, we also looked at the question of whether power and its use can provide us with an all-encompassing explanation for organisational processes and relationships. We decided that it could not. Instead we suggested it is important to be able to recognise when it is appropriate to think in terms of power and in what circumstances that would be misleading. All of this leads to the conclusion that if managers are to use power in organisations effectively, they require a sophisticated level of awareness of what it is and what it can do. This is key to developing a political mindset.

Recapping the line of thinking advanced in the first two chapters, it will be recalled that organisational politics are inevitable because organisations inherently contain individuals and groups with different and competing interests. That is, after all, what we mean by politics – the process of dynamic tension through which competing agendas are resolved. But, as we have said, political activity still tends to exist within a managerial vacuum, even though authority has been overshadowed in contemporary organisations as the primary means of focusing effort. The political mindset is very real but lacks the means of acquiring organ-

isational legitimacy. There is no framework for managerial work based on constructive politics in the sense that there is one intrinsic to rational hierarchy. Or is there?

What we intend to do now is to look at the issues that are raised by thinking of the managerial task as essentially political, and address the question of how a political frame of reference could be incorporated officially into organisations. To do this we will consider the motives that lie behind the exercise of power in organisations, and the problem of whether or not managerial means (power) justify the ends (individual and group agendas). Our discussion will take us into the realm of political theory because it is from there that some of the justification for legitimising organisational politics may come. As the reader will see, there are several parallels that can be drawn between the processes of democratic government and the management of organisations, particularly in the forms that are rapidly evolving in today's business environment.

Motives Are Everything

What lies at the heart of the ambivalence that managers so often display towards organisational politics? For even once they are able to break out of the rational mindset and see its limitations, when they accept the inevitability of competing agendas, the idea of politics as an organising principle causes disquiet. But why?

The most compelling answer is also the simplest. Basic motives. Why do executives play the numbers games, withhold information, ringfence resource, cultivate certain relationships, or engage in any number of unofficial activities that lead to mistrust and disapproval? It is their motives that are at issue. We have questions about their actions that demand some answers. For whom are they doing it? Who will benefit? Above all, what is the organisational justification for their actions? Even if we are not still caught in the mindset of authority, rational economic organisation, and corporate unity, it is easy to draw sceptical conclusions.

Justifiable motives are at the heart of all political activity, not just the controversial variety found in organisations. Think of the doubt that so often surrounds the motives of governments and their elected members. We question whether their manifestos are genuine before we submit our choice at the ballot box. How much of what they say is merely a vote-chasing tactic, an election promise to be forgotten or broken once power is assured? We accuse them of scoring party political points against the opposition rather than addressing the issues of government. The media regularly expose abuses of high office on our behalf, and we are then confronted with the spectacle of 'disgraced' individuals clinging to power, sometimes we believe, at any cost. More fundamentally, we worry that mainstream parties in countries considered as major economic powers appear to be converging on the middle ground, encroaching on each other's traditional political territory, and loosing sight of their core values in the process. It all points to a widespread mistrust and scepticism about the role of politicians, which some commentators now say is a global phenomenon, and fundamentally demonstrates the importance people attach to the worthiness of motives. A deserving and just cause in the service of others is a much easier motive to identify with than one of self-seeking ambition.

A question about the human condition that has long fascinated philosophers and social scientists is how these diametrically opposed motives go hand in hand. Can you have one without the other, or if you prefer, are they but opposite sides of the same coin? It is hard for most of us to understand how either pure selfishness or selflessness is possible, whether it be as a psychological state or as a basis for society itself. We know that both kinds of motives are inherent in most of us, and that the relationship between them is critical to understanding ourselves, and to being a competent member of any social group. Indeed, people who do not possess this balance, being at either limit, are very noticeable members of society. Excessive egotists and do-gooders are marginalised, and at the extreme, both dispositions are recognised clinical conditions. Yet if balance of selfless and selfish

motives is key to psychological maturity and social effectiveness, it can also be elusive. At times we see it neither in ourselves nor in others.

Understanding and being able to achieve this balance is essential to political proficiency in organisations, as is the ability to recognise it in others. This is because clarity about motives is necessary to distinguish between politics that in some sense serve the organisation, and the politics of personal gain or inter-personal rivalry. The political mindset as a legitimate managerial framework is only made possible through this distinction. Without it politics remain discredited by the 'official' model of rationality. Unlike the world of government, where politics are institutionalised as the mechanism of government, there is no such baseline in organisations. In other words, putting to positive use the inherently political nature of organisations turns on the idea that managers are sometimes motivated by worthy causes, that these sometimes conflict, and that just as with the politics of government, this is fundamentally good, not bad.

The Question of Means and Ends

Once a manager goes beyond the rational framework for action and heads for the political arena, the issue of means and ends constantly presents itself. Do the aims justify the methods of achieving them? It is a question that does not arise to nearly the same extent within the rational mindset. Lines of (hierarchical) communication, corporate goal-setting processes, common measurement systems, or statutory decision-making procedures are rational organisation means that managers rarely need to justify using to achieve rational organisation ends. They are more likely to have to explain when they do not use them. In sharp contrast, behind-the-scenes lobbying, pursuing hidden agendas, massaging the figures, or fixing the decision before the meeting, fall within the twilight zone of acceptability. We have deliberately used words like 'massaging' and 'fixing' to heighten the effect. Unless you adopt a 'purist' rational mindset position

and rule all such methods out of court, it is not easy to decide what is justified and what is not. The only other way of simplifying the judgement is to take the 'anything goes' line, which raises too many ethical and moral problems to be acceptable to most managers.

The issue of justifiable means therefore presents a real dilemma. However, it is fully resolvable from within a political mindset because the means are acceptable as essential to the managerial role. Remember that it is only from the perspective of the rational mindset that they are defined as illegitimate. The more that core political processes like taking opposing positions, lobbying, or building support through alliances are seen as *the* way of getting results in the absence of corporate unity, the more the political mindset acquires legitimacy anyway. In that respect the justifiable means problem diminishes, although it does not disappear altogether. The methods can still be abused, and it remains entirely possible to cross the boundary into an ethical and moral hinterland. Where does being economical with the truth (not telling people everything) become barefaced lying, or revealing harmful information turn into treachery, for example? When does calling in favours start to look more like moral blackmail, or cultivating a relationship seem closer to ruthless manipulation? Much depends on individual professionalism and personal codes of acceptable behaviour. But discussing the acceptability of means with close confidants is also crucial in order to compensate for flaws in individual judgement. However, in the last analysis, staying the right side of the boundary depends on clarity of motive and understanding of how to use power wisely.

Politics and the Concept of Democracy

Having discussed the centrality of motives within the political mindset we will now consider the essential nature of politics itself. We do this in order to demonstrate how a well-informed understanding of politics might be used to usher in the political

mindset. So far we have talked about politics as the process through which both governments and organisations function, although its legitimacy is assured only in the former. In fact, within political theory the concept of politics is fundamentally linked to that of democracy, and we must look at both to understand the full consequences and possibilities of managing organisations from the vantage point of a political mindset. It would be wrong to equate politics with democracy because historically there have been political systems that have not rested on the democratic ideal. They still exist, but few would disagree with the observation that there has been a striking convergence around the core principles of democracy in the second half of the twentieth century. This is because democracy has come to be equated in many respects with the concept of the 'good' society, and throughout the history of political thought the central question has always been 'What is a good society, and how is it achieved?'

The democratic ideal is about equal personal freedom to deliberate the aims of a society. The philosopher John Stuart Mill spoke of citizens' deliberation as being the spine of democracy, although not its entire structure. A democratic system has also to assure citizens of the opportunity to choose the basic aims through an equitable process of representation. Representatives then (only) have the role of choosing the means to achieve those aims. The reasoned consideration of moral alternatives, or 'debate' is the method of deliberation, and it is a deep assumption about the nature of advanced society that there will be conflict of aims. Furthermore, division of power always appears as a trans-historical feature of good society because it is indispensable to stable government. An absence of debate is therefore, by definition, problematic. So potent an idea is this that in times when the majority group overwhelms the opposition, and there is a real prospect of degeneration to a one party system, great unease prevails. The ruling party itself will speak of the need for a credible adversary. In a manner of speaking they defend that which they oppose.

Of course the ideals of democracy do not map exactly on to the reality of government. Far from it. There is always dissatisfaction about the system of representation. Some argue that the divisions in contemporary society lead to a power-sharing stalemate characteristic of the 'hung' parliament. The media are frequently accused of influencing election results, and there is the ever-present tension surrounding the power of professional administrators and civil servants to manipulate government. These are but a few of the enduring imperfections. Of special interest to us is the issue of means because it is here that we encounter the realities of debate and the exercise of power. How much in practice do the established means conform to the democratic ideal? For example, in the process of representation, not all debate is public. Transparency is not always a strong feature of the relationships between politicians and powerful lobby groups, institutional leaders or other high profile opinion-makers. It is not even evident in the relationships between politicians in either the same or opposing parties. Or consider the fact that political parties are themselves organisations. Like all organisations, certain members shape policy more than others, resulting at times in the leadership using its power to force dissident individuals to follow the party line. These 'renegades' are expected to vote against their own convictions, and therefore in contradiction with their representational mandate. Or again, what of the career politician who has cultivated and then put to use many friendships on the way to high office? Some would say that it is difficult to reconcile this with moral conviction.

But do these practices really jeopardise the principles of democracy? One of the great challenges of modern government is translating the ideals into workable processes without compromising their essential qualities. It would be very cumbersome and time consuming to conduct all debates in a public forum, for example. The process of government would become suffocated by the very principles it seeks to protect. Establishing positions, sorting out differences and reaching agreements in private meetings is, in effect, an informal filtering process which smoothes the mechanics of decision-making. The latter stages of the public

debate, then, may be best understood as a formal approval process. Significantly, in the organisational context management knows well the difficulties of including too many people in a discussion, especially when the individual starting points are very varied. 'We are democratised to death' they will say with heavy irony. But in the increasingly democratised world of organisations, as in government, limited transparency and privileged access are only acceptable in the process of debate if the motives of those exercising power are trusted. The political realities of the process of government turn on the belief that the motivations are true to just causes and that a deep sense of social responsibility accompanies the exercise of power. Without this the principles of democracy are unsustainable, and the system of government implodes, a reality evident in many socially and politically unstable global arenas.

Our point is that elements of the political process in government, which appear to compromise the democratic ideal, are justified on the grounds of workability. They can be used to corrupt but are not of themselves corruptions. Rather, they represent the accumulated experience of putting principles into practice – '"operationalising" the concept of democracy' in management-speak. Put another way, they are informal mechanisms that complement the formal procedures of government, and that have become institutionalised through widespread use. In the spirit of the ideal they will always be subject to challenge, and the political process of democratic government will therefore continue to evolve. But for all practical purposes the means of democratic politics have long ago gained acceptability.

The Organisational Parallel

We are not arguing that organisations must behave like governments if political means are to shed the stigma of illegitimacy. Nor are we suggesting that organisations need to adopt in entirety the principles of democracy. It is difficult to imagine how the formal system of representative government, dedicated

to carrying out the will of all constituent members, would be a viable model for organisations of any kind. But there is a parallel between the two, especially when we take account of the informal mechanisms of government, a correspondence which potentially lends great weight to political means being given legitimacy in both contexts, not just one.

Essentially the parallel lies in the multi-interest character of both democratic government and organisations. Competing interests and power sharing is in the nature of good governance, but is a contradiction within the rational model of organisation. But organisations can no longer be effectively managed as centrally planned hierarchies, and the movement towards smaller business units, internal entrepreneurial independence, widespread empowerment and participation, as well as both internal and external networks of collaborative relationships, ensures a multiplicity of interests. In consequence, the idea that organisations are composed of 'stakeholders' has aroused much interest, partly because it places managers in the role of serving their 'constituents' to the best of their professional ability – owners, employees, customers, suppliers and community alike. To be sure, businesses still insist that they attend to the creation of shareholder value above all else, but as we noted previously, it is an inescapable fact that management faces mounting pressure to reconcile this goal with that of discharging 'social responsibility'.

This transformation of corporate life has led management theorists to speak of the democratisation of organisations. Some argue that organisations are now so fragmented, and contain within their boundaries so many different interests, that it would be better to think of them as 'corporate communities'. Increasingly, organisation theorists describe phenomena which have no place within the rational model – 'transformational' or 'visionary' leadership at every organisational level, 'hot' groups and 'pockets of good practice' that drive their own agendas with missionary zeal and adopt a siege mentality towards their 'host' organisation, and the eclipse of organisational structure in favour of critical relationships struck

between individuals. They warn that top management can no longer be sole owners of strategy-making, that this process must be just as much influenced by knowledgeable, authority-averse employees who will go and work somewhere else if they do not get a hearing. In fact the role of top management, it seems, is gradually becoming one of grand social design, achieved through mediation of strong interests which exist both within and beyond their organisations. Such shifts in organisational fundamentals tell us that a new model is emerging. At its core is a picture of organisational life in which the principles of democracy determine the legitimacy of managerial actions rather than authority alone.

Seen from within the context of this paradigm shift, it is not surprising that the informal processes of democratic government are also deeply embedded in organisations. They perform the same function of making the formal principles workable. However, it is not yet clear how far the principles of democracy can be transposed to organisations, and those that are implicit in devolved power structures are usually superimposed on the old principles of rational organisation. The tension between them, most apparent in times of crisis when authority tends to reassert itself, leads to confusion and cynicism. This further obscures the functional role of the informal political processes, and the parallel they have with the same (more accepted) processes in democratic government. But a parallel there is.

Comparison of Common Perceptions about Governmental and Organisational Politics

Governmental Politics	Organisational Politics
■ Perceived as legitimate	■ Largely perceived as illegitimate

- Strongly linked to governmental democracy and the management of diverse stakeholders

- Conflict of aims expected and encouraged

- Legitimacy of covert debate

- A positive process in systems of formal representation

- Limited acceptance of link to organisational democracy and management of diverse interests

- Conflict of aims not easily tolerated

- Covert debate considered illegitimate

- A negative process that frustrates efficient hierarchical management

Managers as Capable Politicians

This resemblance between the politics of democratic government and politics in organisations has grown, as organisations themselves have become more community-like, as they have evolved into complex arrangements of co-operating and competing interest groups. Just as with all significant shifts in the structure of society, the changes are imperceptible year by year, organisation by organisation. They are much easier to see in the advanced stages of a social transformation of this magnitude, and until that point is reached the old order appears to prevail. The efforts to maintain corporate unity that we described in the previous chapter amply illustrate this, and the reluctance to see politics as a legitimate dimension of managerial work indicates that there is still great tension between the rational and political mindsets.

Managers who have a clear perspective on this gradual displacement of one mindset by another have a huge advantage.

They avoid the bewilderment and suspicion that naturally accompany lack of understanding of sea change in organisations. They recognise the need to work with a political mindset while taking into account that this is still questionable in the eyes of others. They will understand something of the true nature of power in organisations, and distinguish between constructive and destructive politics, or more exactly, selfless and selfish motives. Likewise they will be able to see the difference between ethical and unethical means of achieving political goals. And in terms of threading their way through the day-to-day practicalities of working with a political mindset, they will recognise the value of heavy personal investment in developing capabilities beyond those of conventional management competency frameworks.

This involves acquiring an enhanced awareness of the agendas and relationships that drive the political process of organisations, and a heightened sense of responsibility about how to use power in the service of vested interests. It requires the development of an interpersonal skill set that makes it possible to manage relationships and information according to political rather than rational criteria alone. Furthermore, because this implies a very different emphasis of time and effort compared with the conventions of the managerial role, there is also a need to acquire a new focus of core activities. In effect, managers must be able to revise and embellish their positions so that political activities are superimposed on, or supersede, official job descriptions and role requirements. We address these capabilities of being a politically effective manager, and the redefinition of managerial work, in the next two chapters.

CHAPTER 4

The Capable Politician

When most of us become managers we discover that it is a harder role to fulfil than we expected. We come to realise why, before we were managers ourselves, it was easy to criticise those already in that position. All those mistakes that we observed other managers making, vowing never to be like that ourselves, suddenly seem more reasonable courses of action. Clarity evaporates before our eyes, and we begin casting around for ground rules to regain some control. That is when we find out that only some of what needs to be learned can be taught – so much has to be acquired through experience. While prescriptions abound, it turns out that they can only be applied generally. What works well in one circumstance fails in another. For management is complex, and we cannot step effortlessly into it as though born to succeed, remaining undaunted by how different it is from anything we have done before. Not most of us, anyway. Usually it is anything but a seamless transition from one position to the next, and our confidence takes a battering.

What a dismaying prospect, then, to contemplate doing it all over again. Yet the difference between rational management and constructive politics involves just that – relearning the managerial role. In fact it is harder the second time around. Not only do you have to unlearn the official model of management, which

was difficult enough to grasp to begin with, but you have to develop in yourself capabilities which are more demanding still to understand, and as if that were not enough, of dubious acceptability. For capable politicians have a mindset that presupposes understanding and skills which cannot simply be bolted on to rational management practices. Of course they usually operate within a rational organisational context, but constructive politicians have learned to roll with this, applying their capabilities in such a way that official management practices are not unduly threatened or compromised.

In this chapter we will try to capture the essence of these capabilities. We begin by considering the *conceptual understanding* you require to be politically effective, by which we mean your intellectual grasp of the political character of organisations. Next we address the more *personal understanding* needed to maintain balance between self- and other-centred motives, reach great clarity about your own worthy organisational cause, and develop a healthy scepticism about rational organisation. *Awareness* of the business environment and the particular political configuration of your organisation will then be our focus, followed by an examination of the *interpersonal skills* necessary to be politically competent in your key organisational relationships. Finally, we will look at the personal development implications of displacing the rational mindset in favour of the political, in other words, what it is that you ask of yourself when you embark on this transition.

Conceptual Understanding

Organisations have been closely studied for over a century, yet theorists doubt that we are close to a comprehensive understanding of them. As the discussion of mindsets in Chapter 2 showed, there are many ways of conceptualising organisations, and the notion of 'mindset' itself reveals their complexity. Managerial behaviour is guided by more than one mindset within the same organisation, each leading to a particular view of

what an organisation is and what it is not. Within the rational
mindset, then, the boundaries of the organisation are well
defined, and control and co-ordination occur within the confines
of those borders through the mechanism of hierarchy. In
contrast, the political mindset provides us with a view of organisations, not so much aligned around unity as driven by a negotiation of stakeholder interests, some of which are outside the
borders. In fact, sometimes it is not that obvious where the
boundaries fall. From the perspective of both mindsets, organisations are understood in terms of a host of concepts like hierarchy, structure, customers, goals, strategies, teams, processes,
or markets. These represent the universal linguistic apparatus for
management, and they give the illusion of capturing the essentials of what is meant by 'organisation'. But each signifies something very different, depending on the mindset of the user.

We will look at several elements of conceptual understanding
necessary to work effectively within a political mindset.

Power and Politics

Let us start with the fundamentals. As we saw in the previous
chapter, an understanding of the multifaceted nature of power is
essential to political competence. Without this perspective it is
not possible to think much beyond organisations as rational entities, governed by hierarchical authority. You must be able to
recognise the complexity of the influence process, separating
clearly what you might want it to be from what it actually is in
practice. In other words, you need to guard against rational
mindset values clouding your ability to see clearly the true
nature of organisational power. This comes in part through deep-
ening comprehension of the mechanisms managers use to influence one another, and of how limited formal authority is in this
regard. The concept of power must be uppermost in your mind
when you contemplate how you achieve anything as a manager.
You only disable yourself if you give it any less of a profile, for

it needs to take pride of conceptual place in your explanation of organisational functioning.

Similarly, unless you understand how power relates theoretically to politics, and the noble quality of political endeavour, you will always be hampered by the rational mindset view of these concepts. After all, without this insight, what would you make of the idea that effective management essentially concerns the principled use of power in service of worthy causes? As likely as not the words would jar because the ideas behind them would seem nonsensical, threatening even. For if caught within a cynical view of politics, you will struggle to recognise deserving organisational causes, distinguish means from ends, or self- from other-centred motives. Above all, to you an organisation will remain conceptualised as a unified entity, rather than a system of pluralistic interests in which there is inherent value. You will fail to appreciate clearly the role of democracy and the fundamental applicability of certain of its principles to the realm of management.

Relationships

You also need a true grasp of relationships to be an accomplished politician. By this we mean that it is essential to understand the concept of a relationship in an organisational context. That is because so much of the influence process is realised through the medium of the relationships which exist between individual managers, played out in various organisational settings, some public, some private. Unless the specific character and significance of these relationships is clear, you will find it difficult either to build them or to recognise when they are at work.

In theory, within the rational model, relationships are role based, that is to say, they follow from the organisational requirement for individuals to interact on account of the workflow design. When two roles correspond in this way the relationship presupposes a set of shared expectations about how each person will act, founded on their respective accountabilities and respon-

sibilities. It never works that way in practice, of course, because we cannot design organisations with the precision needed to eliminate all role conflict or ambiguity. But much more importantly, people do not relate to one another only on the basis of role, a crucial point if we are to understand the nature of relationships from a political perspective.

If you have a lucid picture of your organisation as a political system, then you will see with ease that mutual interest forms the basis of important relationships. To be sure, mutual interest is not the only source of relationships beyond role expectation – friendship or romance, for example, both come into play in organisations – but it is the one that effective politicians regard as axiomatic to their task. Other sources of relationships may be of help, but are not necessary, not even role correspondence. That is why politicians seek out powerful individuals who may share their agenda even when there is no official organisational reason to bring them together. Conceptual clarity about the basis for effective organisational relationships guides their actions.

In this sense politicians know that only some relationships truly matter, for it is in the nature of managerial relationships that most remain superficial, often based on weak role associations. They realise that it is not an end in itself to develop all relationships, partly because some are more politically consequential than others, but equally because it is not in the nature of relationships for each and every one to be personally significant. They may know many people, but they have not the time or mental energy for a large number of high quality relationships in any sphere of their lives. The politician also knows that effective relationships have an emergent quality to them. In other words, relationships change over time as a consequence of shared experience, and need to be maintained lest they decay. Central to their understanding about how effective relationships are built is the role of trust. They know this to be a product of each relationship. Put another way, they realise that trust does not occur simply because two trustworthy individuals choose to work together. The corollary of this is that politicians do not expect to be trusted by those with whom they have only a superficial relationship.

Conceptual understanding of trust is especially important in political relationships. Because it is surrounded by many value-driven sentiments, trust can be a source of great distraction from the realities of management. For example, organisations often set out unrealistically to create 'high trust cultures' on the assumption that trust must be good, no matter what it costs. To add to the confusion, trust takes several forms, depending on the type of relationship it exists within. It most certainly is not a unitary concept. What is meant by trust in a romantic relationship, for example, is not what it denotes in a professional relationship. In the latter it is more likely to be based on perceptions of role competence. In contrast, the basis for trust in political relationships is primarily respect for worthy causes, whether these are complementary or competing, and integrity with regard to means and ends. Politicians consequently understand that it is appropriate to trust their adversaries provided those individuals are well intentioned in a political sense. They know that if they themselves let self-seeking motives take precedence, or cross the line of acceptability with regard to means, then as with all forms of trust, the breaking of it in a relationship is disproportionately catastrophic. In other words, they understand that trust and mistrust are not simple opposites.

Political Mechanisms

Insight into the nature of relationships must be accompanied by a firm appreciation of how political mechanisms operate in an organisational context, specifically lobbying, using stealth, and appearing to conform to formal organisational requirements.

Lobbying is the process of selling and garnering support for your cause. As with governmental politics, much lobbying in organisations is done in private, through relationships, rather than a public forum. Conceptual clarity about organisational decision-making mechanisms is critical to understanding the significance of lobbying, otherwise you will mistake board meetings, company conferences, executive briefings, team problem-solving work-

shops, and a host of other managerial conventions for decision-
making situations when they are not. Managerial decision-
making, in other words, is often a drawn out process that
characteristically occurs out of the public gaze, with only a small
element visible in meetings apparently called for that purpose.
Lobbying is key to influencing the outcome of those decisions.

Stealth is necessary in organisational politics because without
it you may reveal your purposes before it is wise to do so. As
with all forms of competition, formal or informal, there is
nothing to be gained by showing your hand until it no longer
matters to do so. But stealth seems akin to deception, trickery
and even lying unless it is well understood, and for this reason
is difficult to employ effectively without absolute certainty
about its role in the political process. Skilful politicians think of
it as a natural component of the process and therefore experience none of the disquiet encountered by their rational
manager counterparts.

Capable politicians also know that formal organisational
requirements must be met, not ignored, or worse, railed against.
They understand that the rational mindset coexists with the political in most organisations, and that this must be taken into
consideration. Drawing attention to a worthy cause by failing to
clear the conventional hurdles, they would recognise as nothing
short of politically naïve. A clear view of which formal requirements should take precedence is essential to ensuring that political activity is not simply eclipsed by the effort that would be
needed to satisfy them all. In this regard, meeting quantified
performance targets and deadlines is favoured over the many
other demands of formal organisation because effective politicians understand well the role of measurement, its uses and
its abuses.

Pockets of Good Practice

The idea of a worthwhile cause that might emanate from
anywhere within an organisation leads to the possibility that

individual managers may set out to build pockets of good practice around themselves, with or without permission. It is a natural extension of their commitment to creating organisational change, which will not necessarily be confined merely to persuading others of the merit of their agenda. Far from it. In fact the more ambitious the cause, the more likely those managers are to create initiatives, however local and modest, which involve time, money and people. Conceptually this represents the radical political alternative to top-down organisational change, for if senior management lack the vision to sponsor isolated local initiatives, then from within the rational mindset they are, by definition, illegal.

Conceptual clarity about pockets of good practice is critical to their organisational success. The capable politician, setting out to build a 'pocket' will understand that, in the early stages, it can only include a small number of like-minded individuals who share a strong commitment to the initiative. Identification with the cause must be the driving force, secrecy and a 'siege mentality' uppermost in the minds of those involved, and genuine teamwork based on the desire for high standards of thinking and achievement the norm, rather than interpersonal closeness. Similarly, politically astute leaders of pockets know the importance of managing the boundaries closely. A sharp focus on what information is released is necessary until such time as the pocket can protect itself organisationally through the power of its own success. Even then it is key to understand that a pocket can be threatened by senior management appropriation of its achievements, usually by attempting to use the success as a source of organisational learning. With that in mind pocket leaders understand the importance of recruiting a senior management sponsor who will help protect the pocket in its infancy, and smooth its passage into the position of organisational influence if and when that time comes. Above all, effective politicians know that the vibrant activity contained within a pocket can, in due course, help to shift an organisation's centre of gravity. They know too how easily an organisation can extinguish that potential. Such is the nature of political endeavour.

Self-understanding

Just as conceptual understanding is key to resolving confusion of thinking that comes from the overlay of the political mindset on rational organisation, so self-understanding is critical to unravelling the confusion of motives and values experienced in those circumstances. For discovering the appropriate balance between self- and other-centred motives is not easily achieved, nor is a change in attitude towards the fundamentals of rational organisation such as authority, order and control.

Balanced Motives

Politicians are motivated by worthwhile endeavour, defined as working for the betterment of others. Unlike in government, where political agendas are based on alternative social value systems, conflicting worthy causes in organisations are derived from the stakeholder concept. It depends on the ambitions of organisational politicians as to how far reaching are their agendas. Clearly the more limited and local the agenda, the more those directly involved are likely to be key stakeholders. Nevertheless, even in clandestine pockets of practice, leaders must be motivated to work on behalf of their teams, rather than themselves, as the minimum condition for constructive politics. As we will see in the next chapter, taking responsibility for working towards some better common good is central to the motivation of politically able managers.

   Ambition and a sense of responsibility, then, are the key motivations to pursue a political agenda. Everything else that we might think of as 'motivational' for managers is subservient to these. 'Negative' motives like lack of confidence, risk-aversion, or fear of disapproval are overcome through commitment to a worthy cause, while 'positive' drives such as intellectual stimulation or desire for self-determination ultimately tend to be by-products of political endeavour. Yet this certainty of purpose is only possible when managers understand well their own ambi-

tion and sense of responsibility. If this is lacking then it is their very human and entirely legitimate concerns for job security, good bonuses, rapid career moves, or other self-centred motives, that guide their actions. They get caught up in moral dilemmas, issues of personal integrity and feelings of guilt, and risk compromising their credibility as able politicians.

Whether it is the act of pursuing a worthy cause that creates this necessary self-understanding for each of us, or whether it is insight into our own motivation that makes constructive politics possible, is immaterial. It is almost certainly both. Political capability depends on our understanding of where to draw the line between self- and other-centred motives, or to put it another way, being clear about how selfless we are prepared to be. The simplest possible starting point is to ask yourself what you want to achieve in your present managerial role. If the answers you give are mainly along the lines of 'getting promoted', 'keeping your nose clean', 'making a name for yourself', or 'meeting this year's revenue target', then you have probably yet to alight on your worthy cause, and while ambition may be driving you, your sense of responsibility for the betterment of others may need some clarification.

Managers with Attitude

Values about rational organisation run deep. From within that mindset we do not just believe authority, order and control are natural organisational phenomena; we feel with equal vigour that they are inherently positive. And of course they are – up to a point. That point is the limit of their usefulness in the context of contemporary organisational forms we discussed earlier. Yet for the political mindset to flourish a critical perspective on the values that underpin rational organisation must come into play. But how?

The answer is managerial irreverence. Not disrespect and discourtesy, but a healthy scepticism about what is possible through so-called formal organisation. It means adopting an attitude of impiety towards the principles of rationality; scorn and

disdain, however, would be unworthy sentiments. A good analogy is in the way that children, as they develop, discover their parents to be flawed role models of adulthood. But difficult as this insight may be for some young people to reconcile with the image they hold of their parents, it does not follow that they lose respect for them, or for the institution of parenthood. Irreverence and respect can coexist, but in that circumstance respect is no longer unconditional and unquestioning. It is, instead, founded on balanced judgement rather than received values alone.

Such maturity of perspective about the values of rational organisation is essential to political competence, but is hard won. It clearly requires more than being prepared to adopt an anti-formal organisation stance and engaging in subterfuge. Radicalism is not the answer in organisational contexts because revolutionaries are easily marginalised, patronised, and dismissed as incompetents. After all, it is always easier to take an extreme position and vilify your rivals, than it is to maintain a strong position while honouring those who oppose you. Constructive politicians do not attack authority and corporatism but use their irreverence to question and challenge from a position of benevolence towards those still caught in the rational mindset.

Awareness

In Chapter 3 we often suggested that the effective use of power depended on high levels of awareness. In that discussion we were referring to the need to be able to recognise the power bases of other people, the domain of usability of power and when it is being exercised. Able politicians, in other words, have a keen knowledge of their organisational situation. They know who is influential with whom, where and how decisions are made, and what those decisions concern. This knowledge they obtain by actively seeking it, particularly through the political relationship building process we described earlier. Awareness, then, involves much more than simply being alert when in the

company of people you *believe* to be key organisational players. It refers to an active and continuous search for knowledge about the agendas of other people and their effectiveness as politicians, how your organisation functions in decision-making terms and what the important issues are that it faces.

Stakeholder Knowledge

'Who are my most important stakeholders and what are their agendas?' These are the key questions for capable politicians intent on gathering knowledge about who will support and who will oppose their efforts, and can only be answered through extensive personal interaction with stakeholders themselves. Third-party perceptions are insufficient to create this knowledge because they are usually contaminated by those individuals' agendas. To some extent it is a matter of trial and error to determine who has an interest in what you wish to achieve, and it is important to distinguish between those who are interested and those who, from a rational mindset perspective, ought to be interested. Bosses are the best example of where this differentiation needs to be sharpest. The knowledge you build will be indispensable to deciding which stakeholders you need to give priority to, for you cannot devote high levels of attention to them all. You have to choose.

Your stakeholder analysis needs to establish knowledge of the agendas of those within your political field of vision, and the motives that lie behind them. It is, of course, these motives that tell you about the balance of self- and other-centred interests, and how stakeholders resolve the means–ends dilemma. To put it another way, you need to create for yourself knowledge of their ambitions and sense of responsibility. In addition, you must also be able to assess their levels of awareness. If you lack any of this knowledge you will be unable to judge successfully the integrity and political astuteness of your stakeholders, and you risk revealing your own agenda to someone who lacks one or both of these capabilities. This kind of knowledge is therefore essential to minimising the risk in trust building.

Organisational Knowledge

What kind of awareness about an organisation is essential to the capable politician? Primarily knowledge of who makes key decisions and about the decision-making processes. If major decisions affecting you are made by individuals too organ-isationally distant to create a relationship with, then knowing who they are is important to reaching them indirectly where possible, through your stakeholders. Decision-making processes involving several people may sometimes be similarly influenced if you are not included yourself, but you first need to know how these work. They are of two kinds – public and private. The first relates to formal processes, consisting of mechanisms such as boards, executive committees and management teams. Of course these are not usually public in a transparent sense, since the processes are conducted behind closed doors. But they have known (or at least knowable) constitutions, terms of reference, membership, and decision-making criteria, all of which may affect how you should attempt to make a case through either direct or indirect representation.

The private form consists of agreements made between individuals in the decision-making process who have political alliances, and sometimes personal relationships. Some of these agreements are reached literally in private, and some are implicit in the interpersonal dynamics of committees and management team meetings. Awareness of the understandings and relationships between contributors to organisational decisions is essential to positioning your own agenda. Lacking that knowledge you will be unable to work effectively with hidden opposition, or capitalise on a high level of tacit support. Neither is a recipe for effective influence, and may have the added effect of reducing your credibility on account of naïvety. Once again it is relationships with your stakeholders that are the most likely sources of this knowledge, together with oppor-tunistic observation of the relationships between key organ-isational decision-makers.

Knowledge of the Business Environment

Awareness of what is happening in the outside world is critical to knowing the key issues faced by your organisation. It is knowledge that can be acquired both internally and externally, but there is a fundamental difference depending on which source you use. Knowledge originating internally is gained by talking to those who primarily interface with the environment, and to key decision-makers. Using established relationships is less significant than finding occasions on which to ask questions, and if those do not arise routinely you have to create them. Alternatively, read what these sources write. Whatever method you use to gain the knowledge, it is essential to guessing or learning the nature of forthcoming decisions that may affect you.

However, internal sources may be wrong, biased or complacent, and changes in the environment will go undetected or ignored. Supplementing your knowledge through external sources is therefore a good use of energy and time, but needs to be highly focused. Aside from making maximum use of formal mechanisms such as market research or regular customer and supplier interfaces, the key here is systematically to create chances to gain knowledge. These may include anything from attending public seminars, conferences and management development events, to sitting on a professional committee or contributing to an industry-specific forum such as an advisory body. Again, reading is an efficient means of raising your awareness of trends and shifts in the environment, but published material is not a substitute for detailed and intimate knowledge of what is happening in customer, supplier and competitor companies, government departments, public agencies, regulatory bodies, or any other relevant organisations.

In addition to confirming your awareness of critical issues for your organisation, then, external sources may allow you to introduce that knowledge. Presented skilfully, so as not to threaten those individuals whose role is to anticipate developments in the business environment, this has the benefit of developing your credibility internally. It is knowledge that can only be gained

through dedicated effort, but it marks out capable politicians. By one means or another they come to know the important questions to be addressed in their organisations.

Interpersonal Skills

Politicians require the same interpersonal skills in relating to others as all managers. However, because of the necessary emphasis on influencing through relationships, there is a need for certain ones to be especially well honed. These are the skills of presenting persuasively, challenging productively and reading others accurately. They are more correctly described as skill sets because each consists of several core interpersonal skills combined in a specific way. Productive challenge, for example, involves assertive statements, open and probing questions, as well as careful listening.

Persuasive Presentation

The ability to win support for your agenda is determined by your skill in presenting a good argument. Obvious? Of course it is. But less apparent to some managers is the limited potential of their well-written reports and business cases to impress influential decision-makers. Your drafting skills, to borrow an expression from the world of government politics, may be second to none, but unless you present in person you severely curb your chances of success. By 'presenting' we mean far more than addressing an audience with the support of visual aids. In fact this may not feature in your efforts to win support until late in the process, if at any stage. After all, lobbying, especially of the impromptu 'corridor conversation' kind, hardly lends itself to the format of formal speeches.

In seeking to influence others in favour of their worthy cause, capable politicians use a complex skill set. It involves intro-

ducing ideas through suggestion, selective blending of supporting information and making logical connections. This must build towards demonstrating deep commitment and enthusiasm, and at some point usually requires direct disclosure of personal motives. The presentation style should be one of collaboration, win–win, in other words, and demonstrate a willingness to concede where appropriate. This last point is critical to success since effective influence is rarely possible without you giving something to the person you wish to sway, impress or inspire. Above all, your language and use of voice need to convey respect for the view of the other, and the possibility that it conflicts with your own. This is central to the principle of constructive politics.

Productive Challenge

The most economical way to challenge other people is to tell them you disagree with or disapprove of them. You do not need to exercise much skill, it takes little time, and they know where you stand. However, it is usually ineffective with influential decision-makers, and has a long-term negative effect on your relationship with them. Challenge is critical to dislodging the organisational status quo, to influencing attitudes, beliefs and habits, and in pursuing a political agenda, is often a valuable complementary process to persuasive presentation. But to be productive more is required than head-to-head provocation.

A far more effective process of challenge is to use what interpersonal skill experts refer to as 'causal analysis'. It is a method of using questions to *cause* others to *analyse* their assumptions, views or behaviour, and is essentially educational in nature because it implies personal changes, willingly undertaken. To be successful it must be used in conjunction with very active listening, because the answer to one question should determine the content and format of the next. Since serial questioning will sound like an interrogation, no matter how benign or well intentioned, there is also a need to inject assertive statements into the

process, together with a demonstration of empathy for the other person's thought processes. In addition, a touch of humour and a little self-deprecation by the challenger can have a disproportionately positive effect. But it requires great skill and careful timing, especially when challenging those who are partially aware of what you are trying to do. It is actually easier to use with the highly aware because they are more likely to appreciate the value of the process and apply it themselves.

Accurate Reading of Others

Every action of capable politicians needs to be underpinned by sound reading of the motives of others. This is presupposed by persuasive presentation and productive challenge, but occurs independently of those processes. It should be continuous, both active and passive, direct and oblique, but always unobtrusive. As we have said, *motives are everything*, the basis for all thriving political alliances, and they are the final criterion for judging your stance in relation to each of your stakeholders. Since they have a range of selfish and other-centred aims, and varying degrees of willingness to reveal these, you cannot afford to be lax with vigilance. Those who are other-centred and open may be guileless at times, but they are not problematic. Neither are self-centred individuals who are easy to read because they (can) do little to disguise their motives. It is the poker faced whom you have to work much harder with in order to judge them well, otherwise you may err in either of two wrong directions. First you may misread reticence about revealing intentions as a sign of self-centredness, and second, statements of other-centredness may appear sincere when they are not.

Accurate reading requires constant sifting for information contained in what others say and then do or do not do. Because it does not only depend on data from conversations in which you are a direct participant, reading can often be informed by passive observation alone. It is key to compare words to subsequent actions because of the rich information this linkage contains

about intentions, although it is not of course final proof of either self- or other-centredness. Reliable reading also requires that you understand well your propensity for either cynicism or seeing the best in people, since both can distort your conclusions about the motives of others.

Constructive Politics: An Overview of Key Capabilities

Conceptual Understanding

■ Power and politics: evaluating the complexity of the influence process and the role of motives.

■ Relationships: evaluating the different barriers for organisational relationships.

■ Political mechanisms: recognising the value of lobbying, stealth and the adherence to formal procedure.

■ Pockets of good practice: appreciating the value of establishing worthwhile causes to stimulate organisation change.

Self-understanding

■ Balanced motives: clarity about personal and organisational motivations.

■ Managerial irreverence: a healthy scepticism about the limits to what is possible in formal organisations.

Awareness

■ Stakeholder knowledge: knowing the agendas and motivations of key players.

■ Organisational knowledge: knowing who makes key decisions and how they are made.

■ Business environment knowledge: knowing the critical organisation issues.

Interpersonal Skills

■ Persuasive presentation: developing collaborative outcomes through personal enthusiasm, suggestion, logical connections and the disclosure of motives.

■ Productive challenge: causing others to analyse their assumptions.

■ Reading others: a continual observation and evaluation of the motives and actions of others.

Personal Development Implications

Some managers are natural constructive politicians. For most, however, becoming an effective politician involves a difficult learning process. As we have seen, there are layers of capabilities from conceptual understanding to interpersonal skills, all holding significant personal development implications. Mastery of each capability in its own right requires time, energy and devotion to the task. As with all complex learning it is understandable to falter, to lose the will to persist. But above all it is a hard personal journey because this transition is about acquiring a mindset, and there is a powerful counter force – rational organisation.

A shift of mindset only occurs when there is sufficient dissatisfaction with the prevailing one. It is the same with any significant personal transformation. Negative feelings have to exist in order to overcome the pull of familiar, tried and tested ways of thinking, or skills and knowledge you have learned over many years. There is a lot to lose. Only when there is enough disillusion, frustration, feeling of injustice, or similar opposing motiva-

tion, will a transition occur. And it will be an uncomfortable experience, characterised by pendulum emotions that accompany success and failure as you struggle to learn in an environment which is anything but supportive. For in demonstrating ineptness as a fledgling politician you risk bringing the might of rational organisation down upon yourself.

But the prize is high. Successful personal transitions tend to culminate in a feeling of great achievement, a higher level of maturity, and those who discover the organisational potential of the political mindset have a sense of new found liberation. Their self-belief spirals upwards. However, these outcomes are only possible because the development process is emotionally arduous and motivated by disaffection with rational management values. To put it another way, such a transition cannot be just an exercise in intellectual stimulation. So if you have got to this point we believe you need to ask yourself a question before proceeding to the next chapter. Here it is:

> *What are the negative feelings you harbour*
> *about rational organisation that will allow*
> *you to succeed as a manager far beyond its*
> *limitations?*

It is a straightforward question and you must be able to give a simple answer. If you can then read on, and we will describe for you how capable politicians operate so that you can take the next transitional steps.

CHAPTER 5

Working With Legitimate Politics

Chapter 4 described the competencies and personal development necessary for managers to become politically able. In order to turn these ideas into action this next chapter examines how managers might work in practice from the perspective of a political mindset. It encourages readers to rethink their role and to work in very different ways from the conventions of managerial activity. Our starting point is to describe what managers actually do now, and why they do it that way in the first place. By examining the evidence that researchers have amassed in their studies of managerial work, we will be able to compare and contrast activity patterns based on the rational mindset with those of the politically astute manager.

The reader will be presented with a series of case studies describing everyday managerial work. This will enable us to illustrate the ways that managers operating within a political mindset use their time, channel their energies and prioritise their work. It will also allow readers to compare the use of their own managerial time, and how this may need to be changed to reflect constructive political behaviour and motivation.

In the final part of the chapter we will show how managers can simultaneously work with the value of rationality and the reality

of a political environment to secure operational and strategic change in the interests of their organisation.

Understanding What Managers Do

The analysis of managerial work has a long tradition. Identifying, cataloguing and classifying the roles, tasks and activities that managers actually spend their time on has been a preoccupation of academics and practitioners for many years. The main focus of this enquiry was very much set by one of the earliest researchers, Henri Fayol, who in 1916 classified the management role into eight basic functions: determining objectives, forecasting, planning, organising, directing, co-ordinating, controlling and communicating. Down the years the Fayol classification has been developed and elaborated many times over, taking into account different variables such as national culture and organisational constraints. However, most of this work has been concerned with description and classification rather than with an effort to build theory. Put differently, we have learnt more about what managers do than why they do it.

Despite this, the impact of these descriptive studies in reinforcing the rational nature of managerial work has been immense. For the most part, the rationality of organisations is taken for granted – in other words, the researchers have an implicit theory of managerial behaviour. There is a broad assumption that managers act as neutral professionals, exercising their expertise with impartiality, while the impact of power has been largely ignored. For example, Henry Mintzberg, the author of another landmark study into managerial behaviour in 1973, classified management in terms of ten different roles, each being derived from formal organisational authority and status. In other words, Mintzberg's managers were assumed to be motivated to enact their roles in accordance with their formal organisational authority.

Attempts to develop alternative approaches have mostly focused on empowerment and its constituent elements of trust, openness and collaboration. But as we noted in Chapter 2, these concepts still reflect the core principles of the rational model because they are embedded in values of corporate unity. Realistically speaking, the decentralisation of power and authority is the management response to an increasingly unstable business environment, rather than a genuine desire to release decision-making authority, driven by the recognition that unity is a myth. This is never more evident than during times of downturn when top management feel compelled to return to traditional command and control measures in order to turn round ailing corporations.

In order, then, to locate political activity from a theoretical point of view, we will next consider the motivations that drive managerial behaviours, focusing on responsibility, the common denominator to all managerial work. This will enable us to illustrate how patterns of everyday managerial activities are driven by motivations other than the desire to conform to the principles of rational organisation, and allow us to avoid the self-fulfilling nature of tacit, value-driven theory.

So Why Do Managers Do What They Do?

The differing motivational assumptions that lie behind the rational and political mindsets are particularly well illustrated in the concept of managerial responsibility. Colin Hale, a management theorist who has written extensively on issues of managerial work, identifies organisational responsibility as the defining element of management work and one that distinguishes managers from non-managers. This being so, when we ask basic questions as to why managers feel responsible, to whom are they responsible, and for what, we begin to reveal the true motivational basis for their actions.

Motivation and the Rational Mindset

In the rational mindset, organisations are economic units created to achieve shareholder value if they are businesses, or in the case of public institutions, realise specific social objectives with minimal use of resources. In this way organisations are constructed on the ideals of efficiency and effectiveness and managers are the agents through which these ideals are implemented. Objectives that contribute to the overall strategy are cascaded down to individual managers who are *given* specific responsibility for the success of the collective endeavour. With this responsibility comes the formal authority to pursue their organisational goals. Rationally, then, managers are motivated to exercise their power responsibly in the interests of the wider organisation, the team, the function or the business unit.

But with responsibility also comes accountability. Managers are answerable for their own actions and for those of others, not just direct reports, but in today's organisational structures, for individuals and groups in cross-organisational arrangements of many kinds. They are faced with the dilemma of individual accountability for a collective outcome, and a very basic dilemma this is. For while responsibility for collective interests is axiomatic, 'imperfections' in the rational model throw up the twin problems of aligning the 'irresponsible' agendas of other managers, and the behaviours of those who do not have to act responsibly since they do not have organisational responsibility in the first place. The more trying these problems become, the greater the test of managerial motivations, since from within the rational mindset, responsibility fundamentally means working to create alignment.

Naturally enough, the understandable response to these motivational challenges is to dig deeper into the tool kit of rational craftsmanship. Take the example of Carlo:

Carlo had worked in furniture manufacturing all his life and risen to the position of operations manager. In this new role he was being asked to contribute to the wider strategy of his company, and work more with colleagues across the business, not just those in manufacturing. He soon found that they had different agendas to him, and in due course this started to weigh him down. He failed to persuade them to give greater priority to certain manufacturing issues that seemed to be holding back the entire company. Consequently, he lost interest in the bigger picture issues and focused down into his own direct area of responsibility. That is where his effort should be going anyway, he reasoned, and he set out to drive through improvements he could control. He knew every little detail of what was happening in production, and would constantly get involved with the work of his staff, telling them what they should be doing and how they should be doing it. He didn't see that he was interfering since his motives were purely about improving the efficiency and effectiveness of his operation. Inevitably there was a back reaction, and he was met with a whole string of further problems such as mysteriously disappearing resources, and a sudden upsurge in unreliability of tried and tested technology. He worked 60 hours a week but didn't move his facility forward at all.

Faced with the problem of extending his responsibility beyond his immediate remit, Carlo's reaction was to reach for the conventions of rational management. When these failed him he had to retreat in order to affirm his responsibility and identity as a manager. This too became counterproductive, but it allowed him to close off the contradictions of the rational mindset, and to maintain purity of motive.

Motivation and the Political Mindset

Politically fluent managers are guided by a different set of assumptions about organisations because they understand the limitations of the rational mindset. They have the same basic needs for security, recognition and advancement as everyone else, but the political mindset leads to a definition of responsibility that bears only passing resemblance to the one we have just described. Capable politicians have a heightened awareness of the responsibility they are given but, crucially, they also take responsibility. Just as the rational manager looks to the pursuit of corporate goals through assigned responsibility, competent politicians define their own goals and seek to take responsibility outside of their allocated remit in order to achieve them.

Politically able managers recognise the fallacy of pursuing corporate goals without acknowledging the significance of self-interest. They will be quick to appraise projects and assignments that have little chance of success, whether they are corporately aligned or not, avoiding them in favour of more realistic alternatives. They are more likely to feel responsibility towards a select group of like-minded people who share a common organisational agenda. In practice this means that their focus of responsibility may move as different projects take priority, and will require some negotiation. Above all, they see responsibility in terms of worthwhile effort on behalf of others, and there are times when this runs counter to corporate unity and the organisational status quo. The example of Kate helps put these ideas in context.

Kate is an organisation development director who has acquired a firm understanding of the political perspective through her role. The culture of her company reflected a

priority towards the sales divisions, and other functions in the business tended to see themselves as reactive operations that added less value. The role of her particular function had mainly been to provide basic training. Kate realised that this culture was creating an 'order chasing' business strategy which looked increasingly limited and dangerous. So as well as 'doing training' she began to spend time and energy on organisational development initiatives that cut across the culture.

She identified those mangers who she thought could really make a difference to the organisation and spent large amounts of her own time helping them achieve significant results for the company. What has now started to happen is best described in her own words: 'I get a real buzz working with these managers. We are working on some big strategic issues that are sending out some shock waves across the company. It's a small but powerful network and I think we are really getting somewhere. We have to negotiate all sorts of political minefields and because I have encouraged them down this route I feel a real commitment towards them. Not so much their teams really, I don't really know that many of them personally, it's just the leaders with whom I enjoy working.' And her conclusion? As she puts it: 'Because we are working somewhat against the conventional ethos of the firm I have to spend a lot of time networking, making sure I put a positive spin on our work. It's too easy to get squeezed out if senior management don't think you're "one of us".'

Today Kate believes she still has much to do but is finding things easier because people see her as a key player who asks questions about important issues. She has developed visibility and credibility with a group of influential managers.

This case illustrates the motivation of politically competent managers to take responsibility rather than work with what is given. Kate was motivated to do this because she recognised that she has a realistic chance to achieve something worthwhile. By working with a group of like-minded people she has been able to promote her own interests, and those of the organisation. Notably, though, not all of the senior management would agree (yet) that she has the overall business's interests at heart. She clearly feels responsibility towards her small group of 'co-conspirators', and this commitment appears to be to them as individuals rather than to the larger groups they represent. She was, and still is, critical of the business strategy, but recognises that acceptance of it diminishes rather than promotes her influence. Through the political process she has attracted greater levels of influence, but recognises that this is bounded by the extent to which she is able to establish a legitimate agenda for herself through her networking and relationship management.

In this section we have used the idea of managerial responsibility to highlight the different motivational assumptions that lie behind the political and rational mindsets. Carlo, working from a rational frame of reference, was motivated to take responsibility for activities that promoted organisational alignment. When these good intentions faltered in the face of differing interests, he chose to close off the frustrations that this caused by focusing on those few activities where his motivations could remain true. Kate, on the other hand, working with a political mindset was motivated to move beyond what was given, to take responsibility for activities that were understood by the organisation to be outside of her area of control. She was motivated to do this because she felt that she had a good chance to achieve something worthwhile for her company. Clearly, these different motivations have fundamental implications for the day-to-day activities in which managers engage.

Activity Patterns of Constructive Politicians

What in practice, then, do managers do when they act as constructive politicians? We will try to show the reader how to think in terms of activity patterns that reflect this, and to do so we will use a series of case studies. This will allow the reader to observe directly where managers operating from within a political mindset focus, what they give priority to, and how these priorities are executed. Three pairs of cases will be examined in this way in order to be able to compare the activities and motives of the politically capable with:

■ The rational manager, who believes he or she is working to the goal of corporate unity

■ The destructive politician, whose goal is self-interest and organisational power

■ The disempowered manager, who has come to believe that individuals make no difference to organisations.

Each pair represents a direct comparison of two managers addressing the same role or type of role from different standpoints. Using these three perspectives we hope to present a comprehensive picture of how constructive politicians contrast, not only with managers of a rational persuasion who eschew politics, but also with those who perpetuate the negative image of politics, and those who feel themselves to be victims of Machiavellian intrigue and deception. A short analysis of the motives and activity patterns of the characters will follow each pair of cases.

Pairing 1

Corporate Unity and Constructive Political Influence

VICE PRESIDENT – MANUFACTURING *North America*

The role of the North American Operations Vice President (VP) in this international manufacturing organisation reports through to the country CEO. There are manufacturing operations in several other countries that need to collaborate on joint projects but are also competing for long-term work allocated from the corporate centre. They have been using lean-manufacturing principles for some time now.

Don – The Rational Approach

Don (see Figure 5.1) has been VP Manufacturing for four years now and in the company for just over ten. On the face of it he has many of the qualities required for the position. He has good analytical skills and is well respected by most of those who work for him. He's a hard worker always leading by example, 'mucking in' when there is a crisis or emergency. His old boss, who appointed him but retired 18 months ago, was always quick to praise his knowledge of the manufacturing facilities and his ability to get things done on the shop floor. It was his old boss who gave him his nickname of 'get it done Don'. However, Don now has a new boss brought in from outside the group and he now feels much less comfortable that his contribution is as valued as it used to be.

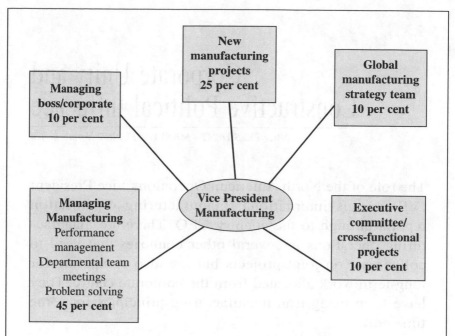

Figure 5.1 Don – the rational approach

'One of my enduring principles of managing in any company is to keep the boss sweet', said Don. 'That means always delivering on your key objectives and trying to be a team player. I put a lot of time into making sure the shop floor runs to capacity and in the most cost efficient manner.' In essence this is Don's number one priority. He spends around 45 per cent of his time keeping the factory going and has a good reputation for meeting production targets. He is loyal to his team and works with them sorting out difficult production problems, and is often seen on the shop floor talking to his supervisors. 'I feel responsible for my production workers, they have a hard job and I need to do my job well if they are going to do theirs well.'

However, despite this focus Don has struggled to get on with his new boss. Don feels that Derek doesn't seem sympathetic towards the difficulties he faces in meeting his

production targets. For example, he is often asked to spend time on group policies that he sees as being disconnected from the reality of conditions in the plant. 'Derek just doesn't seem to understand the constraints I have to operate within. There are the unions for start off, huge amounts of policy from group, the cost structure I'm saddled with and so on. I do try to stick to these policies and procedures but this creates all sorts of problems for me and my team.'

In addition he attaches considerable importance to formal hierarchy which often has the effect of narrowing his options even further. As he puts it, 'I don't actually have very much latitude for all my seniority, and Derek doesn't represent my corner at group very well. Some of my problems need the full attention of the Group President of Manufacturing, but Derek never really tackles him on these. Basically I don't really understand Derek, and so I don't trust him. I guess if I'm honest, I try to stay out of his way if I can.' He pauses, and then continues, 'However, if I do get caught by Derek with something or other he wants I always ensure it gets my full attention.' Don spends nearly 10 per cent of his time responding to such requests, but because of his mistrust of Derek, he shies away from trying to build the relationship.

Don also has a reputation for running a tight team and is a stickler for well-managed departmental meetings. He has put a lot of time and energy in recruiting and developing a team that thinks and acts in the same way in the belief that this will ensure consistency. 'I remember when I first got appointed to VP' reflected Don on one occasion, 'I realised just how unfocused the team was, that they were not pulling in the same direction and were far too involved in projects way outside of their brief. I really had to force the group to get things done to deadline. I would listen to their ideas of course, but then gently and firmly let them know what I was thinking. This led to big argu-

ments, and our meetings used to last all day. But after about six months of hard graft and some plain talking from me, they are much more focused. I know there is a bit of "OK Don, I hear what you say" sometimes, but basically we now all see things the same way.'

Organisational politics really annoy Don. He sees them being entirely to do with 'internecine conflict'. In the Executive Committee he hears his colleagues squabbling about turf issues, but tends to see the surface content of these 'squabbles', distancing himself from the discussion. As he explains, 'Sure, if they want to know my opinion I let them have it, but otherwise I let them argue until they are blue in the face. It washes over me. Derek really needs to get a handle on this kind of stuff. He needs to provide much stronger chairmanship at these times. The trouble is none of them really understand manufacturing, and I should have Derek's support, but I don't get it.'

Don finds similar difficulties on the Global Manufacturing Strategy Team. It only meets four times a year but Don sees it as being of limited value. He has to prepare a considerable amount of information each time, but does his best to minimise the time he spends on this. He 'gets away' with about 10 per cent. 'The amount of information these guys require is amazing', he says. 'They are always trying to prove that their sites are performing better than the rest. My operation is usually above half way up the league table. Some of my colleagues reckon we should be at the top, but those guys in Korea don't have my union problems to contend with. There is a lot of politics at these meetings too. I try to collaborate but it is difficult when they don't see the priorities we have to work with. Like when they wanted Jimmy Carlson to visit the Korean plant to show them how we reconfigured the line for the HNS product. I wasn't trying to be difficult. It's just that I needed him at the time for SAP. And

as we are the pilot site for SAP for the whole group we needed to take priority.'

Don is well respected for his technical knowledge and expertise and his boss knows that he will ensure that MRP2 and SAP will be implemented on time and with a fine attention to detail. He devotes around 25 per cent of his time to these operational projects but very little to strategic issues. As Derek says, 'Don does a good job, he's conscientious, he keeps the plant working effectively and I can always rely on him in a crisis. It's just that ... well ... he's blinkered, not very sophisticated. I wish he represented our interests at group more adroitly so he doesn't keep coming up against so much opposition. And he's too easy to read, it's easy to press his button, just criticise his operations and see the reaction ... instant action! He may have reached his limit.'

Dave – The Politically Capable Manager

Dave (see Figure 5.2) is starting to really enjoy the job. Having taken over from Don 12 months ago he is now relishing the freedom it provides. He found the team he inherited somewhat lacking in initiative so to begin with he spent quite a bit of time finding out what made them tick. 'They are pretty good at keeping the operation running so I let them get on with it. Consequently I now only spend about 25 per cent of my time on day-to-day manufacturing activities. I also found out the team were actually quite innovative under their layer of cynicism, so I've been keen to get them working on different projects, freeing up about a quarter of my own time to work on more strategic projects like the supply chain. The production levels are never going to improve until we get the

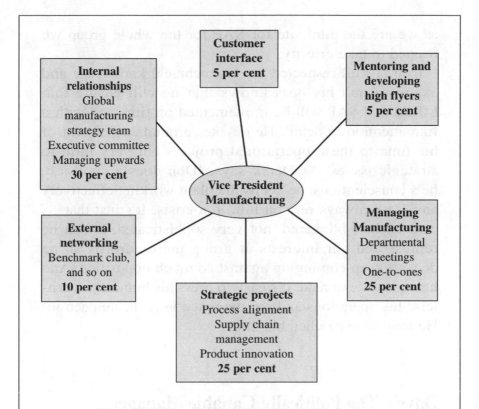

Figure 5.2 Dave – the politically capable manager

supply chain issues sorted out. The Korean Manufacturing VP has proved to be a great ally here because he has the same problems with the centre's approach to logistics. Together we've been able to out-manoeuvre the VP of Group Logistics. Not that I would trust the Korean guy with my life you understand, but on this one we have some mutual advantage.'

This comment reflects a substantial difference in Dave's approach. Nearly 30 per cent of his time is devoted to networking with global manufacturing contacts and senior managers. It was through one such ad-hoc conversation that he picked up a valuable piece of information. 'It was only by luck that in chatting to Mark

(VP of HRM) that I found out that Derek and the VP Group Logistics go way back. Would you believe it! I thought, "Christ, I'm going to have to keep quiet about Korea." We presented the supply chain improvement initiative as a *fait accompli* once we could prove the benefits. I had to put a hell of a lot of work into managing the boundaries with the guy from Korea. It involved a lot of one-to-one conversations, really eyeballing people so they knew where we stood. Derek had a tough time with his friend Mr Logistics and was pretty angry until he saw the numbers.'

Once his team realised Dave's intentions, some of them felt insecure with the strategy they were developing. Worse still, most of them were initially so poor at forming their own opinion that Dave had to hold himself back from providing all the answers. This meant that he had to work hard to balance his own motivation to get things moving with the longer term need to get real commitment from his team. For example, before one of the monthly production meetings, Dave had told everyone about his thoughts on some changes he thought they should make in certain areas of the production process. 'Now I knew some of them didn't like it because they were worried about quality. So I asked Jim Carlson to submit an initial paper to the meeting. The more he worked on it the more he saw the advantages. But everyone knew I was in favour of it so the danger was that given their history, they'd just roll over because I was the boss. At the meeting I said, "OK what are your thoughts about Jim's paper?" Silence. I repeated the question, but this time directly at Gerry Greenberg. He gave me some ambivalent response, which was followed by several of the others. So I said "Look you guys I am not making this decision on my own. I want your thoughts." Anyway, Jimmy took up the baton and we had a good discussion, the result of which I still think was

an error – we put off a full review of component manufacturing until next year. The upside, however, was that the
quality of our meetings pretty much increased after that.'

For Derek, Dave has also been a breath of fresh air in
the Executive Committee meetings. He is particularly
good at recognising the strategic issues and ensuring they
are surfaced and resolved. Because he spends around 15
per cent of his time with customers and external networks
he has brought a much wider perspective to discussions,
and is able to support his ideas with reference to external
benchmark data. In fact he usually gets what he wants at
these meetings because he spends a lot of time talking to
the rest of the executive before and after each meeting.
'It's my iceberg principle' says Dave, 'I reckon at least
two-thirds of the work around the executive meeting
needs to be put in one on one. Almost the least important
part is the meeting itself.'

Like Don, Dave found that Derek played things a bit too
close to his chest at times, but once Dave had delivered on
a few difficult jobs and had demonstrated an ability to take
a strategic view of the business, Derek was much more
open with him. 'The thing about Derek is that you have to
understand what makes him tick. As long as he can demonstrate he is ahead of the game at group he's much happier.
Because Derek is a salesman at heart he is happy if he
thinks that the Group Manufacturing President is keeping
an eye on me, while the group guy thinks Derek is
managing me. I suppose I kind of implicitly encourage
this, after all it gives me room to focus on much more
interesting stuff like product innovation.' In this way Dave
often gives the appearance of complying with corporate
policy even though he sometimes has his own agenda.

Dave is always on the lookout for new ideas; he likes
people who can think outside of the box. He regularly
volunteers to mentor and support people on development

programmes because he extends his network and identifies like-minded people who can help him. 'Some of their ideas can be pretty wacky, but there's this guy in procurement I'm working with at the moment ...'

Analysis

What can be learned from Don and Dave's motives and resultant activity patterns? How do they differ? Take Don, whose motives appear laudable. He is concerned for his team and the business, working hard to support the corporate line, while adhering to policies and procedures to ensure consistency. He thinks that he is acting collaboratively in the interests of the group and is being helpful to his manufacturing counterparts in other plants. He knows he doesn't really trust his boss but nevertheless tries to be loyal upwards even though this causes him considerable problems. He has a respect for those in seniority, but believes in using his authority downwards.

However these qualities are marred by Don's lack of interpersonal and business awareness which leaves him vulnerable. For example, he seems not to understand the misuse of his authority with his team, and their reaction to it. Similarly, he appears unaware of the way that divisional and group colleagues are manoeuvring around him in the Executive Committee and on the Global Strategy Manufacturing team. He recognises that others are politically motivated, but dismisses them as people who distract from broader business issues. His lack of personal awareness also left him vulnerable to Derek's political agenda.

Don's response is to dive down into the (safe) detail of his operations in the belief that this will enable him to add value. He concentrates on local activities and on

managing the here and now of manufacturing. Consequently he doesn't really collaborate with other areas and even restricts resources like Jimmy Carlson being shared across the group. In this way he is engaging in political activity too, although he himself would not see it that way.

Relationship building seems restricted to hierarchical routes, upwards to his boss and downwards in his team. He only spends 20 per cent of his time on this activity in comparison to over 50 per cent allocated by Dave, who extends his networking within and beyond the group. The political significance of the global team is largely lost on Don and there appears little motivation to learn from this group. Similarly, Don's developmental work, which occupies 25 per cent of his time, is focused down into the business. Consequently he has become inward looking and overfocused on his own priorities. Once again, of course, Don himself would not recognise this. In fact he would be stung by the criticism and find it difficult to accept.

Unlike Don, Dave recognises the difference between personal and organisational interests and is able to use this insight for the benefit of the company. Because of his thorough understanding of others' motives, there is a risk he may appear manipulative, but this is kept in check through his high self-awareness. For example, he recognises the danger of misusing authority with his team, even though his personal style would allow him to push decisions through faster. He develops trust selectively by relating this to specific projects and personalities. For example, he only trusts the Korean VP with regard to their one shared project, and on this he is prepared to work covertly.

In consequence, Dave has a very different set of priorities to Don. He is deeply interested in relationships inside and outside his division, and in the agendas of key people around him. He is able to build support for contentious initiatives like the logistics/supply chain project. He

recognises the constraints that manufacturing is faced with, but unlike Don, sees a way of tackling these by looking for collaborative alliances. Paradoxically, while Don believes he is focusing on the best interests of the company by ignoring politics, it is Dave who actually accomplishes more by working with competing and mutual interests.

The resulting activity pattern is very different from Don's. Much less time is spent managing the day-to-day manufacturing activity – only 25 per cent in comparison to Don's 45 per cent – and much higher priority is given to relationship management inside and outside of the company. Although like Don, Dave allocates 25 per cent of his time to projects, he focuses more on issues that have a wider organisational impact, and beyond the boundaries of his own division. In sharp contrast with Don, he has a real interest in innovation, and is prepared to make time to challenge convention by working with other nonconformists who can provide different perspectives.

Pairing 2

Personal versus Organisational Motives

COUNTRY MANAGER, MWC *Netherlands*

The Dutch Managing Director of MWC reports directly to the Regional CEO in this global IT systems supplier. He sits on the European Country Managers' Forum. The role encompasses all aspects of business unit manage-

ment, but because there is no manufacturing facility in the Netherlands, most of the focus is on sales and marketing activities. The company has a strong sales-led culture, and most of their business involves putting together substantial IT system projects where there is a need to integrate product from other hardware and software suppliers into their solutions.

Gerard – Destructive Politics

Gerard (see Figure 5.3) has worked for MWC throughout his entire career. He joined as a graduate trainee and has spent most of his time in sales working his way up through pre-sales, professional services and account management for one of MWC's biggest customers. Even though he is now the MD of a significant operation he still works extensively in his old sales area because he so enjoys it. His justification for this reflects a deep insecurity. 'Not that I would openly admit this to any of my colleagues, but I reckon I still spend around 35 per cent of my time selling and talking to customers', he confided. 'This is a sales-led organisation and as long as I keep my contact with major customers I stay in touch with what is going on in the market and help close the high profile deals.'

However, even though he has only been in the MD role for two years, he has still accomplished a substantial turn-around for the Dutch operation by introducing a radical reorganisation for the business. The reorganisation reduced costs by nearly 15 per cent but created a lot of pain for the business unit, which was felt for months afterwards. 'I know the reorganisation created a lot of discomfort, but I'm not being paid to be liked in this job', he

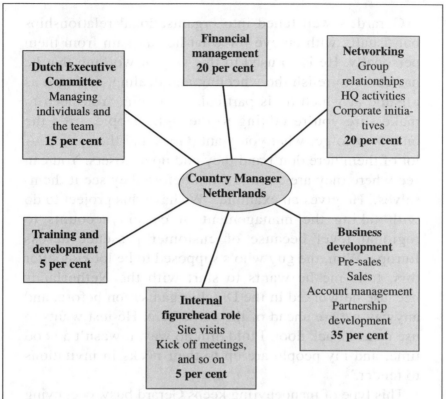

Figure 5.3 Gerard – destructive politics

says. 'I was under a lot of pressure from region to improve performance, and although my plans met with questions from the senior team in Holland, we had to get on with it. I've known most of them some time, and I know what their pressure points are. So I can usually get them heading in the right direction, although in one case I had to put a guy on special projects. Around here that is one step short of being shown the door.' Not surprisingly, this attitude led some of his senior managers to believe that Gerard was only interested in conformance with his own aims, and was prepared to manipulate any dissent out of the way.

Gerard is well tuned into organisational relationships but usually with an eye for what he can gain from them personally. He is so used to this way of working that he has come to relish the wheeling and dealing, seeing it as a game at which he is particularly adroit. 'You need to make sure you're talking to the right people – it's the only way to get what you want. Go round the system. A lot of them here don't and they end up as losers. You can see where they are coming from before they see it themselves.' He gives an example. 'We have this project to do with taking the management of certain accounts to regional level because of customer presence across Europe. Wim, the guy who's supposed to be looking after this, tells me he wants to start with the Netherlands because he worked in the Dutch organisation before, and anyway we are ahead of the game here. He just wants to use us as a back door. I told him no way, it wasn't a good time, and my people are up to their necks in invitations to tender.'

This type of manoeuvring keeps Gerard busy, occupying as much as 20 per cent of his time. He knows it creates enemies, but he believes that delivering the required revenues makes him invincible. 'You've also got to look after the numbers. At the end of the day it's the numbers that really count. But it takes a lot of time, about a day a week but it's worth it. I make sure we are absolutely watertight on the details. I know some of our people complain it takes nearly three weeks out of every quarter to put the reports and presentations together, and then follow up on Charles's questions (the regional CEO), but once we have the okay nobody can touch us.'

Gerard's approach to problem solving involves using blame to generate action. For example, given advanced warning that the customer satisfaction survey would contain some strong criticisms of his organisation, he

called in the relevant parties for a 'learning review'. No one thought for one moment that it was going to be about learning, and in the meeting no one accepted responsibility, Gerard accused everyone of a cover up, and each area represented blamed the other. He appeared to feign amazement afterwards, remarking to several who had been present, 'No wonder we have got into this situation when you fight among yourselves like that.' It is an outcome that typifies the game playing mentality of the destructive politician. Those caught up in it then resort to their own games, looking after themselves at the expense of all else, and contributing to the downward spiral of the self-serving motivations that reinforce the illegitimacy of politics.

Inica – Constructive Politics

Inica (see Figure 5.4) took over from Gerard after he was promoted to become European President of Marketing. He left just before the publication of the annual customer and employee satisfaction survey that showed a marked decline in performance. Gerard blamed external pressures for the downturn, but Charles confided to Inica that it was clear Gerard's approach was not appropriate for a long-term growth strategy.

'When Charles told me he wanted me to take over from Gerard, my first reaction was that I was not up to it, and anyway I don't trust Charles. The Dutch operation is male dominated and I thought "I don't need this – I'm not the right person." But I waited and talked to various people, and started to feel better about it. At least I knew the personalities and the politics after working all that time with Gerard.'

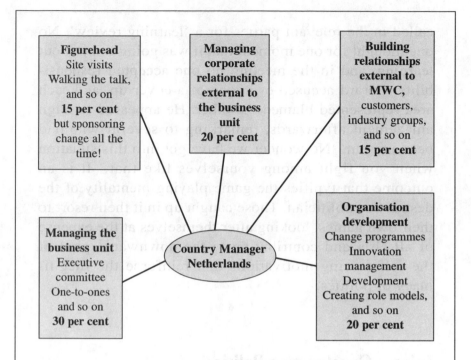

Figurehead
Site visits
Walking the talk,
and so on
15 per cent
but sponsoring
change all the
time!

**Managing
corporate
relationships
external to
the business
unit
20 per cent**

**Building
relationships
external to
MWC,**
customers,
industry groups,
and so on
15 per cent

**Managing the
business unit**
Executive
committee
One-to-ones
and so on
30 per cent

**Country Manager
Netherlands**

**Organisation
development**
Change programmes
Innovation
management
Development
Creating role models,
and so on
20 per cent

Figure 5.4 Inica – constructive politics

As one of Gerard's protégés, she initially tended to apply many of the tactics she had seen him use. 'I took up where he left off – "divide and rule" I suppose he would call it. I was met with real defensiveness, and because I couldn't deal with it I got directive when people didn't do what I thought we had agreed. But they always found some way of letting things fall off the agenda. The initial goodwill extended to me vanished, and I was getting nowhere. None of the executive team seemed capable of collaborative working and Charles was breathing down my neck.'

'Eventually I confided all this to Wim. He is probably one of the few people I really trust in the company. His reaction was to the point. He simply said, "You have made

a poor start". I think that was something of an understatement. I thought I knew the personalities but I'd made too many assumptions. It was a good conversation, but basically what he told me was "Just back off and find out what people are thinking. Try showing them you are willing to do something for them." This became a real turning point for me.'

Over the next few months Inica's behaviour changed substantially. She spent a lot of energy talking to people in her own operation and in the European organisation. She became increasingly good at using time to build relationships – for example, travelling with Charles, who, she discovered is much more receptive to ideas once settled in Business Class with a glass of wine. She now uses any meeting or chance conversation to find out about other people's agendas. 'I've been amazed just how much information is out there for the taking if you stop indulging yourself in your own assumptions. Don't get me wrong, I've not turned into some altruistic angel – that wouldn't get me anywhere in MWC. I do it so I can achieve something.'

Inica's network of relationships across the European region and into the US has become a source of considerable influence for her. For example, one thing all her fellow country managers agreed on was that the quarterly review was unnecessary. It was far too retrospective and detailed. In her conversations with colleagues, Inica built up a strong lobby group who were willing to raise the issue at the European Country Managers Forum. She knew Charles would be completely opposed to the proposal to abandon the quarterly review so she kept it quiet. At the meeting he was out-voted.

This degree of influence could not have been achieved without the credibility of a substantial improvement in operating performance behind her. As a consequence of

her extensive relationship building inside the Dutch operation Inica was able to make much greater headway in initiating change. Gerard had stripped the organisation to the bone and removed most of the initiative with it, so Inica needed to build this up carefully. She encouraged pockets of change and when they started to succeed, she built them up as examples to the rest of the Dutch organisation. Not all of them made progress, of course, but they were nonetheless publicly rewarded if they exemplified behaviours she believed were needed to move the business unit forward.

'In retrospect' she says, 'my behaviour at the beginning seems obviously unsophisticated, but when you're caught up in the middle of the storm it's hard to understand. I guess the feedback from Wim helped me see I was only thinking about my issues, and if I wanted to get people to move I had to find some common ground with them. It's an uphill struggle, but it gets easier. I still have to think carefully about who I talk to about what, but I feel much more relaxed now.'

Analysis

On the face of it Gerard and Inica appear to display a number of similar priorities. They both spend time getting to know people, assessing their agendas and motivations and both can see through the veneer of corporate rhetoric as to how decisions are really made in MWC. They both seem to possess a wide network of contacts and try to keep track of shifting power distributions. Indeed there is a great deal of similarity in the way they spend their time. Neither is afraid to use the power that their position brings in order to achieve results. They also recognise the importance of

managing their boundaries to ensure the most favourable interpretation of performance. In consequence, both are very powerful individuals.

The central issue that distinguishes Gerard from Inica is that of motive. Throughout the narrative it is clear that Gerard is focused primarily on promoting his own interests above those of his colleagues and the business unit. He has come to see the organisation as a political arena in which there are winners and losers, and that staying on top requires working the same way himself. Over time he has become too ready to read negative self-interest into the behaviour of others, and this validates his own approach. These motives encourage an activity pattern that focuses on staying one step ahead of the game. Time and energy are spent soaking up the gossip that enables him to stay in control. As his managers remove their goodwill he becomes even more controlling and manipulative.

In contrast, Inica's motives lead her to find a balance between her individual and organisational interest. She has clearly undergone a significant transition, triggered by Wim's feedback. This has enabled her to understand more about her own motivations and aspirations, and to develop a genuine interest in the motivations of those around her. In the process she herself appears to have become even more motivated because she can see how to get results in the prevailing culture, and is prepared to work hard for others who show the enthusiasm to follow.

Particularly noteworthy is the way she uses her time to develop political maturity. All conversations and even business trips are an opportunity to understand others, lobby her cause or communicate her vision. Such an approach requires high standards of thinking, in terms of personal clarity about her role, her motivations, and the way her organisation works. This requires a better use of time rather than more time. Consequently she devotes 20

per cent of her time to positioning her business unit at corporate levels. That is augmented with 15 per cent of her time allocated to maintaining an external perspective, not just with customers (unlike Gerard), but with partners and industry groups as well. Some 30 per cent of high quality time is devoted to working with her team, collectively and in one-to-one relationships, helping them get to grips with the changes she believes to be necessary.

Pairing 3

The Value of Individual Action

MANAGEMENT ACCOUNTANT AND IT DEVELOPMENT
MANAGER, KIX BUSINESS INFORMATION *UK*

The Management Accountant reports to the Financial Controller in this UK-based subsidiary of a European business information company. It produces a variety of hard copy and electronic marketing, credit, legal and financial reports. The Management Accountant manages 25 staff.

Colin – The Disempowered

Colin (see Figure 5.5) joined KIX four years ago from a competitor company. He had always worked in finance, mostly in management accounts. When he first arrived he was very enthusiastic, and set about revising and streamlining the monthly accounting procedures. He related well

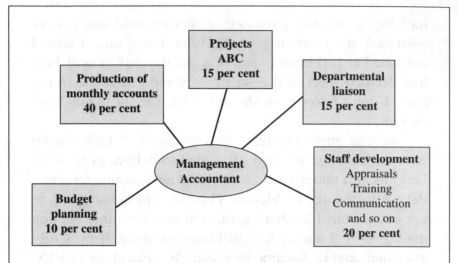

Figure 5.5 Colin – the disempowered

to the collaborative culture of the company and tried to support colleagues in the other areas of finance. The business then went through a difficult period. Technology was fast reducing the cost of standard business information reports that had previously attracted a high margin, and prices were being forced down. There was a corresponding knock-on effect in terms of headcount, and Finance had to reduce staff numbers.

Colin came up with the idea of creating a multiskilled resource pool to be shared by the finance sections, as each had different peaks and troughs over the month. The idea was not received well by his colleagues who said they were concerned about the way this would limit operational flexibility. 'I worked hard on putting a plan together', said Colin. 'Jack (the Financial Controller) had said we should discuss the situation among ourselves and recommend where the staff cuts should be, so I offered to give it some thought as a start. Pat (Credit Control Manager) didn't buy it and she would not budge. At the

meeting to discuss it we agreed that I would talk it over
with Jack the following week. When I saw him it turned
out that Pat had been to see him the day before and Jack
had decided most of the staff cuts should be made in my
area. I don't know how she did it but she did a good job
on him.'

'You can guess the rest', he continued, 'I took the hit
with the cuts and we have struggled to deliver ever since.
Jack doesn't understand and thinks I am incompetent, and
Pat walks about like Mother Theresa. I'm never going to
get caught out like that again.' Pat and the other section
managers in Finance had little co-operation from Colin
after that, and he became increasingly cynical about KIX,
seeing hidden agendas all around him. He buried himself
in management accounting routines, spending up to 40
per cent of his time driving for complete accuracy in the
work of his section. Information was divulged grudgingly
to business managers, he harangued the IT Department
constantly because of system failures, and was quick to
blame anyone who did not meet his high standards. He
initiated no new improvement projects, and worked on
those that were assigned to him with just the minimum to
get him by – perhaps only 10–15 per cent of his time
being used in this way. But the more he withheld information the more people would go around him to Jack, or
ignore him altogether. This only served to confirm
Colin's cynical view of his colleagues and their self-
interested motives.

Over time, this resulted in Colin being drawn deeper
into the belief that there was little he could do to change
the situation. Doing nothing, of course, only served to
confirm this for him. Typical of his view is the response
he gave to the Information Systems Manager (Steve), who
had been attempting to persuade Colin to go with him to
speak to Jack about some expenditure on system improve-

ments in Management Accounts. 'Why bother?' was his attitude, 'You can't change his [Jack's] mind, and anyway, he is being driven by the FD.' Steve's suggestion of getting the support of one of the business managers (Christine), who he knew was frustrated by the lack of IT development, was met with much the same air of resignation: 'There's no point. She can't help. It wouldn't achieve anything – just more hassle.'

But the more Colin focused on his own agenda to defend himself, the more vulnerable he became. In time, the business managers he was there to support used his unwillingness to help as a political brickbat with which to complain to Jack. Colin received poor performance appraisals and was passed over for promotion. He became more isolated still, which reinforced his perception of the unfairness that surrounded him, and his own powerlessness to change it.

Steve, Information Systems Manager – The Principled Use of Power and Stealth

The IT Development Manager reports to the Technical Director and is responsible for all software development on existing and future programmes and applications. Steve therefore has a significant role in new product development, an area critical to the company's success.

Steve (see Figure 5.6) started with KIX two years ago and was seen as a breath of fresh air in Information Systems. The existing operation had become a scapegoat for line management failures, and morale was low. Most of the best people had left, yet software development was critical to the future success of the company. At the outset Steve talked to his internal customers about the service

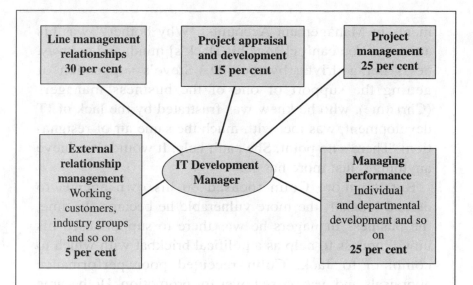

Figure 5.6 Steve – the principled use of power and stealth

levels they were looking for and the issues they had. He also spent a large amount of time talking to his team, finding out about their aspirations and competence levels so as to get a match between what his customers wanted, and what his team were able to deliver. By then he was well placed to draw up a plan repositioning IT Development as a much more strategic contributor.

An analysis of the workload of the department showed Steve that 75 per cent of the projects they worked on were operational: most of them were concerned with small incremental improvements to the core information databases. Very few could be considered strategic, and most importantly, there were no high value projects that would enable KIX to regain its competitive advantage. 'We were not up-front about the plan we agreed in the team. I knew that any substantial changes from operational jobs would be a problem for most of the business managers. They talked about business improvements but when it came to it they had a short-term view so we still had to maintain a

basic database support service.' The team decided it best to keep certain ideas hidden until it had made some progress. For example, they did not reveal that they had a development project being worked on at the concept stage with the help of external consultants, or that three of the team attended business school IT strategy seminars. The expenditure was assigned codes that would not arouse suspicion, and the team agreed cover stories that would suffice unless close questions were asked. In the event of more intense scrutiny it was understood that Steve would handle the situation.

More openly, Steve and his team made it their goal to challenge the assumptions upon which existing IS projects were based, asking what sort of return a project was expected to produce, and how each one related to business strategy. These questions attracted both negative and positive responses, the latter coming from certain of the business managers frustrated at the lack of IT development. One in particular, Christine, who managed the legal information market, turned out to be doing some clandestine work of her own. It was limited in scope, but Steve was naturally keen to help her once she had opened up to him about it.

Realising that there was scope to build support for himself through pockets of like-minded people in the business units, Steve began to use these opportunities systematically, but always informally. For example, he was able to cross-charge for the use of outside contractors to cover development expenditure that he would have struggled to justify, and could not have hidden. The outcome was a number of small but significant projects that improved the profitability in two lines of business.

'Only then did I start to broadcast what I was doing', confessed Steve. 'Jeremy [Commercial Director] was hooked, especially by the figures from Christine. He wants

us [IT] involved in several areas on business improvement projects, so I'm using him to persuade Mike [Technical Director] to go with this, and give me more resource.'

'Not all the initiatives work of course', says Steve. 'You have to be philosophical about it. I tried to get Colin interested in some work in his area. It didn't happen. I never made it past trying to get him to go with me and talk to Jack. I even suggested getting Christine to talk to Jack from the business point of view. She could have helped him [Colin] but he was not interested. There's no use flogging a dead horse and Colin is pretty dead. I doubt if he will survive here but it is not my problem. There are too many other things going now, and if people don't want to get on the bandwagon, they lose not me.'

Steve's position has improved steadily to the point where he has gained the confidence of most business and support function managers. He has double the budget allocation that he began with, and there are major IS development projects in most areas of the organisation. It is widely accepted that he will succeed Mike, who is due to retire in two years' time. Although Steve has some ideas about repositioning the role of Technical Director to be more customer facing, he judges that now is not the time to voice these.

Analysis

When Colin started at KIX he had little understanding of the political nature of organisations. In responding with sincerity to the espoused values of a collaborative culture, he followed the familiar path of working in the collective interests of the business. But he failed to see how politics shape collaboration. Experience did not match expecta-

tions, causing him to spurn the school of rational thinking in favour of the school of hard knocks. The low awareness of individual and organisational issues that caught him out in the first place continued to reduce his power and influence. He could not see how or why people circumvented him; he knew only that such 'underhand' action created injustice, reinforcing his own limited view of what was then possible.

The resulting pattern of activity is once again inward focused but on this occasion motivated by defensiveness. Some 40 per cent of Colin's time is spent micro managing the historic monthly accounting information and only 10 per cent on the wider forward-planning aspect of his management accounts role. He believes nothing can be really changed in the organisation so there is no point in trying to do so. Steve's encouragement to be proactive falls on deaf ears and, in effect, Colin has disempowered himself.

In contrast, Steve is optimistic that he personally can make a difference, although this is tempered by a critical insight into the power issues within the organisation. Given the prevailing culture he recognises that there is a need to present an appearance of conformity in order to ward off interference. Similarly, he remains quiet about his overall intention to reposition his department, but that means managing the boundaries between his department and the business carefully, finding influential like-minded allies with whom to make his plans work. When he is sure he has built up the requisite support and achieved some degree of success, he is then prepared to leverage the power he has gained to stimulate further change.

A high level of drive encourages him to view the boundaries of his influence as widely as possible. If there is an impact to be had on product development, Steve is interested. He doesn't restrict himself to IT. Yet even with his

high ambition, Steve is very realistic about what is possible. He doesn't waste further time on Colin, nor does he lose sight of his department's central role in keeping the databases up and running. This balancing act is essential in maintaining his credibility.

Like Dave and Inica, Steve appears able to balance personal and organisational interests. He readily shares his own agenda with those he trusts, and sometimes takes risks with those he is unsure about, like Colin. The result is a high degree of consistency in his behaviour that seems to allay suspicions about his motives. And again like Inica and Dave, this ability to balance personal and organisational concerns is built on a clear understanding of his own motives, the interests of others, and key business drivers. The resultant activity pattern is focused on relationship building throughout the organisation and beyond. Around 45 per cent of Steve's time is spent building relationships both inside and outside of KIX. This is particularly important given his functional support role, and contrasts sharply with Colin, who only spends around 15 per cent of his time on those same activities. Steve invests time in getting his team behind him, using management development opportunities to widen their perspective. That achieved, he only needs 25 per cent of his time to manage the department. Colin, in contrast, requires 40 per cent of his. Steve is therefore able to focus a quarter of his time on projects and political activity that have a wider strategic relevance for him, for those around him and the company.

The Complete Constructive Politician

These case studies reveal how far managerial work may differ from the accounts of well-ordered, neat activity described by many of the management theorists. While these important

contributions were made at a time when organisational environments were much more stable and predictable, and organisations
more centrally controlled, it is doubtful that they ever really
captured the essence of managerial work. So what can we learn
from our six case studies about the way that politically capable
managers use their positions to be effective in contemporary
organisations?

What we will say in answer to this question is based on one
overriding conclusion about the activity patterns of politically
able managers – they see their role as one of continuous change
management, unlike their rational mindset counterparts. In the
rational model, change tends to be seen as a process of moving
from one stable state to another, in other words, as a discontin-
uous process. That is because change takes the form of initiatives
driven by top management who periodically set about making
organisational improvements, often in response to crises precipi-
tated by the business environment. As a result, change has come
to be viewed as an additional activity to the main task of
managing, and a common response when confronted with new
change management responsibilities is, 'But how am I supposed
to fit all this in to my normal work?'

For politicians, managing change is not an activity scheduled
in for half a day each week, but something that is synonymous
with the task of management. However, it would be easy to
minimise the importance of this insight. Readers may be tempted
to respond: 'Of course my job is about change. I live with
change everyday.' That is undeniably true, although it has to be
said that most daily change is trivial. But it misses the point. For
what distinguishes the politician's view of change is the ambition to shape an organisation through his or her own agenda, and
it is the pursuit of this that is ceaseless.

Establishing Worthwhile Causes

From a political perspective, strategy, operational activity and
change are the result of negotiation between vested interests that

emerge over time. To exempt oneself from this 'messy' arrange-
ment is to exempt oneself from power and influence. Progress is
only made in organisations because individuals like Steve, Dave
and Inica are prepared to put effort into promoting worthwhile
causes, and considering those of others. Like Colin, if managers
wait for top-down, unambiguous direction, or assume that power
vacuums provide long-term safety, they are implicitly passing
power over to others. If they have no agenda, one will be defined
for them. In activity terms this means that able politicians give
priority to seeking out like-minded individuals with whom to
establish value-adding projects and causes. This has two important implications for their activity patterns.

■ *Stimulating organic change.* As organisations become more
  interconnected and complex, people naturally tend to see the
  greatest worth in local issues because these affect them most.
  Able politicians recognise the value of local self-interest in
  stimulating change. It was the basis on which Steve worked
  with his department to reposition its role. Groups that initiate
  change in this way have been variously labelled as 'hot
  groups', 'communities of practice' or 'pockets of good practice' by contemporary management writers. They may
  conform to formal organisational boundaries and divisions, or
  at the opposite extreme, consist of informal networks of like-
  minded people spread throughout an enterprise or across
  several. As with Steve and his move to reposition the IT function, these groups feature influential individuals who share a
  common purpose, with or without formal organisational
  consent, and tend to adopt a siege mentality.

  Managers like Inica use their time to establish such pockets of
  good practice as exemplars and role models for organisation
  change. This may involve encouraging others directly to work
  covertly, and protecting them until it is time to use their
  achievements in the broader organisational context. It amounts
  to an organic process of change that stands in marked contrast
  to the rationality of top-down transformation.

■ *Stealth and the nominal adherence to accepted procedure.* In pursuing worthwhile causes that run counter to formal policy and procedure, managers inevitably risk being taken for maverick individualists. Maintaining credibility is, therefore, key, and astute politicians appear to comply with formal procedure. It requires the principled use of stealth, exemplified in the way Inica gathered support to abandon the quarterly review, or in the tactic Steve took in maintaining a basic database support service when his real priorities lay in new product development. This requires careful boundary management by all involved in a pocket of good practice, and might include such 'dubious' practices as defending office space, limiting access to reports, or being selective about who attends key meetings. Such practices are of course close to the edge of constructive political behaviour, and can only be construed as principled if those involved are able to justify their actions in the interests of the organisation.

Relationship Building

If the capable politician is motivated to take individual responsibility for worthwhile causes with other like-minded individuals, then relationship management is the vehicle through which these are negotiated and implemented. This requires a particular activity pattern that clearly distinguishes the work of politicians, and it is determined by the manner in which they build relationships up, across and outside the organisation.

■ *Managing upwards.* Conventional wisdom emphasises the importance of boss and subordinate establishing common expectations, a free flow of information, compatible work styles, and honesty, while gaining senior management buy-in for change is central to the rational model. However, from a political perspective this advice can be problematic. True, bosses are normally stakeholders for subordinates, but there is no guarantee that they have the best interests of their direct

reports at heart. Furthermore, organisations are now config-
ured according to processes, projects, networks, and matrices,
and boss–subordinate relations can become indistinct 'dotted
lines'. Bosses may have very different agendas to their 'subordinates'. So one way and another, telling your boss, or other
senior managers, your intentions may be neither necessary nor
prudent. This was the case for Steve; his boss was focused on
maintaining the databases, but Steve saw his real responsibility in developing new software solutions. If your boss has
interests that cannot be reconciled to your own, stealth may be
inevitable unless or until the relationship develops.

Managing upwards is an activity aimed at creating the space
necessary for independence and self-determination. Equally it
can be used to great effect in getting support and sponsorship
from key stakeholders, and in the rational model this is the
starting point for change. However, in the political model,
spending time on this has to be considered in the light of
motives, aspirations and power. Seen this way, the boss is a
potential ally, but may be no more than another relationship to
be managed.

■ *Internal networking*. With increasing organisational complexity,
managers have been encouraged to form extensive organisational relationships. In the rational model, motivations for
networking are about enhancing the co-ordination of effective
operations. In activity terms this means building close
relationships, sharing resources and tackling projects collaboratively. Not surprisingly, networking is often used as a justification for executive development events. Supposedly,
seminars and workshops help managers from different parts of
a business 'to get to know each other better', but what this
often hides is the fact that networking is pursued as much for
reasons of self-interest as it is for organisational co-ordination.

Networking is the motor of political fluency. It enables
managers to generate support, identify key issues and locate
resistance. For the capable politician, the network provides

access to power up and down the organisation, and establishing one's self as the informal link between different networks offers great scope for influencing. Building a network demands an activity pattern that defies the conventions of time management. Dead time becomes prime time – travelling, for instance, can be an activity in its own right. So can corridor conversations, attending 'boring' formal functions and ceremonies, or doing favours – in other words, any situation that can be used to good effect in the effort to understand the agendas of others, and begin to reveal your own.

■ *External networking*. Building relationships across external boundaries is coming to assume an entirely new significance as organisations are increasingly bound to each other through supply chains, joint ventures, strategic alliances, shared processes and resources, and several other 'mutual destiny' mechanisms. In these arrangements stakeholders in organisations may be powerful allies. They can support an initiative if it has a business implication for them, and this opens up further possibilities for the politically minded in realising their agendas. In fact the greater the mutual destiny that exists between organisations, the more politicians think in terms of belonging to a web of organisations rather than to just one. But even where organisational boundaries are maintained in traditional style, there is much credibility to be gained in possessing an external network.

The implications for managerial activity patterns are clear. The able politician devotes time to networking with customers, suppliers, competitors, industry groups, professional and academic bodies, consultants, and other institutions and agencies in the external environment. There is a practical question of where to draw the line, for these are all potential sources of political support, information, knowledge, and if all else fails, employment. Rational managers will draw it tightly round the organisation, dealing only with those in the environment they are 'supposed' to, while politicians will choose on the basis of relevance to their agendas.

In Conclusion

We believe the defining characteristics of the politically fluent manager that we have described here are very much a reflection of the capabilities that are required to operate successfully in today's organisational environment. For if organisational forms and business models are fast becoming unrecognisable in terms of the principles of rationality, that is because the old model of organisation is no longer applicable. These sea changes are leading towards a world in which organisations cannot be managed other than by accepting the inevitability of organic, bottom-up change. The conditions in which constructive politics become the natural means of managing may be rapidly appearing, and it is to this possibility we now turn in the final chapter. Are we soon to see the legitimisation of organisational politics?

CHAPTER 6

Politics – The Essence of Organisation?

We have set out to position politics as a central dimension in management, and we have surfaced the influence of the deep-seated rational mindset in undermining its legitimacy. As with governmental politics, the constructive value of organisational politics stems from the possibility of acting on principled causes, which itself turns on the balance of self and other interest. The moment managers stray from the straight and narrow of the rational mindset, they are faced with the problem of finding that balance. Yet this is their day-to-day experience. It is the essence of organisation and it leads us to recast the managerial role as that of 'politician'.

Maybe it is more accurate to say that politics are *becoming* the essence of organisation. For perhaps the rational mindset was once both the legitimate and entirely dominant one. After all, the more powerful a mindset, the more it saturates our attention. Or has the political dimension always been a serious contender? It is well known that those who have studied organisations for the past 50 years or more have consistently encountered what they called the 'informal organisation' – an alternative mindset, in other words – and managers seem to have always recognised that organisation charts do not fully

reflect power structures. However, the informal organisation is probably better understood as a reaction to control, than as a means of expressing worthy causes. Just the same, we are left pondering whether or not politics, constructive politics that is, have always been a significant dimension of organisations. Perhaps not, given the overwhelming impact of rational values on society at large. We cannot really know. We can, though, be in little doubt now about the power of the political mindset, and the weight of its alternative status. So – is its significance increasing? Will politics become the essence of organisation, the legitimate companion, rather than illegitimate alternative to rationality?

We think so, and in this final chapter we will try to show why. The argument goes like this. The trend towards organisational democratisation, driven by massive changes in the business environment, provides the basis for an organisational model in which the role of hierarchy is severely limited, but which cannot be realised without the legitimisation of political activity. Yet in the face of a long established rational mindset, how realistic an expectation is this? It depends. Clearly education has a part to play, but then education is often instrumental in perpetuating the dominance of the rational model, particularly in the field of management development. How influential education will be, therefore, warrants some conjecture here. But if the institutions of education cannot expose the strait-jacket of rationality, because they are unable to extricate themselves from its values, then it will be the intervention of individual managers, and their ambitions to create enlightened organisations, that will have the most impact on legitimising organisational politics. They will do so only if they see it as personally meaningful and relevant, and *that* depends on them pursuing worthy causes. For it is the pursuit of political agendas that reveals the political mindset as the essence of organisation. There is no limit to the potential for individual action, but it could be a slow process.

The Democratisation of Organisational Life

There is always great debate about the future of organisations, their structure, form and role in society. Central to this discussion is the idea of democratisation, by which is meant the widespread distributing of influence in organisations. This is a process through which a multiplicity of stakeholders become involved in the management of an organisation. It arises both by design and as a consequence of the evolution of organisational forms. Democratisation is based partly on the acceptance that organisations function far more effectively when their internal dynamics are treated as markets, rather than centrally planned economies, and partly on the recognition that organisations are not sovereign entities that can operate independently of their environment. Consequently organisations need to manage themselves in a way that reflects the relative power and value of their range of stakeholders. It is a conception of organisation that reflects directly the mindset of constructive politics because it explicitly endorses the need to take account of internal and external interest groups, while refuting the idea that superordinate judgement is concentrated around the top of a hierarchy, no matter how flattened.

An Accelerating Process?

The move to redistribute organisational influence has a long history, traceable in Europe, for example, to feudalism. In recent years democratisation has become evangelised by business gurus and politicians as a new paradigm of economic, social and political organisation. While there are divergent views about the nature and form of democratised organisations of the future, there is some agreement that they are likely to share the following characteristics:

- Devolved power and responsibility for many more organisational decisions, leading to smaller, self-organising units.

These are likely to operate jointly in corporate structures more akin to a federation or holding company than a uniform entity.

■ Processes that recognise the importance of satisfying diverse internal and external interests, and that emphasise power as a function of successful relationships rather than structure.

■ People strategies that provide for greater levels of psychological ownership of organisational activities, and that depend more on individual contribution, knowledge and leadership.

However, if these ideas have taken root at all, it is not because of well-intentioned words. Rather it is a response to the very real business imperatives we discussed briefly at the beginning of the book, namely, technological advances, the drive for innovation, the impact of globalisation, and an increasing concern for business ethics. These drivers of change have encouraged the democratisation process in several ways:

■ The need for continual innovation and improvement has led to the recognition that individual tacit knowledge, held in the heads of employees and deployed through key organisational relationships, is a rich vein. This has stimulated greater interest in the relative value of individual contribution and generated a multitude of methods to identify, communicate and exploit this knowledge for organisational benefit. In particular, it has led to a focus on knowledge management, and the importance of releasing knowledge to those closest to organisational problems. As information is increasingly disseminated, so organisational democratisation is enabled.

■ The recognition that customer satisfaction is critical to organisational success has facilitated the idea of employee empowerment. In an effort to increase responsiveness to customer needs, decision-making has been pushed down the organisation. Similarly, the intention behind delayering is to accelerate decision-making processes. In other words, these changes are designed to ensure that information, power and

authority are pushed to the point where they can have greatest value for the customer.

■ The benefits of managing knowledge and reducing hierarchy are realised through attracting, retaining and developing key talent. Central to this is the need to understand the motivations of these exceptional people. In response, organisations have increasingly been making determined efforts to create a new 'psychological contract' with employees. In the words of the social philosopher and business commentator, Charles Handy, they are treated as 'members of voluntary clubs' rather than organisational assets, or human resources. In particular, this necessitates providing greater autonomy and choice for individuals so that they can achieve results in ways they see fit. In certain industries, particularly those associated with IT, organisations have had no choice than to treat employees as voluntary members, because their skills and competencies are so much in demand. These changes have the effect of raising the voice of individual contributors in organisational decision-making.

■ As organisations align ever more closely with the needs of specific customer groups, individual business units and departments serving customer segments inevitably become more specialised. For example, the competencies, systems and structures required to run a high street retail bank network are very different from those needed to ensure a successful web-based banking operation. The resulting fragmentation of organisational structures drags organisational power away from the corporate centre in the service of specialised customer needs.

■ The inescapable interdependence of organisations, their suppliers and competitors, has led to increasing acceptance that external stakeholders influence decision-making. This is not just an issue of corporate responsibility but equally one of competitive advantage. For example, the more companies are able to build close relationships with customers and suppliers,

the more effective their supply chain becomes. In some industries, like biotechnology, product development may be
dependent on a knowledge network of thousands of scientists
located all around the world. Democratisation, therefore, is
also being driven by the need for organisational boundaries to
be permeable and, at times, altogether removed.

■ The need to secure greater levels of employee commitment
  has led organisations to democratise their approach to rewards
  and ownership. Many have introduced stock ownership plans,
  albeit restricted to specific management levels, and some
  organisations, like the UK-based John Lewis Partnership,
  include all employees as owners. One hi-tech company values
  its business units on an internal stock exchange to allow all
  employees the chance to purchase 'stock' in sister business
  units as well as their own.

■ Lastly, the democratisation process has also been influenced on
  a global scale by growing legislation in the areas of employee
  protection, participation and communication. Whether this is
  through the establishment of works councils, collaborative
  trade union involvement, profit related pay, or race and gender
  equality, each piece of legislation in some small way provides
  greater emancipation from hierarchical control.

All of these trends reflect the increasing importance of many
voices in the effective management of contemporary organisations. They act incrementally on society at national and global
levels, edging organisations closer to accepting the need to
reconcile different aims as the basis for managing.

Organisational Democracy and Organisational Politics

Clearly these influences alone do not create sufficient
momentum for a mindset shift towards the democratisation of
organisations, for when overlaid on to the rational model, the
result can be frustration and alienation, not emancipation.

Furthermore, attempts to superimpose democratic principles on organisations can devalue the good intentions of top managers and, worse still, generate cynicism about their motives.

For example, ideas of empowerment have often been imposed on sceptical middle managers, leaving them insecure and vulnerable because they are unsure about their future role. The same can be said of attempts to get employees to deposit their tacit knowledge on corporate databases because they can see little personal benefit from doing so. Similarly corporate stock options appear to motivate primarily those who feel they can influence the stock price, usually senior management. Attempts to value employees as corporate citizens by enhancing their employability fall into disrepute when training and development budgets are slashed in the face of poor trading performance. Much the same tension arises when organisations talk of independent business units and then impose a top-down budget process. We could go on. The point is that these kinds of frustrations are now part of everyday managerial life. Evidently something more than good intentions or the changing business environment is required to effect a fundamental redistribution in organisational influence.

Throughout this book we have sought to show how constructive politics are essential to effective organisational functioning, and it is but a short step to suggest that they are also critical to realising the democratic principles necessary for new economy organisational forms. So rather than rely on the gradual gathering of democratic momentum, we would ask the reader to think about how a shift of mindset towards legitimate organisational politics would accelerate the process of democratisation. In fact, there is a more fundamental consideration still in that the democratisation of organisations will only truly arise once politics are legitimate. For it is constructive politics that provide the essential process for reconciling the differing interests endemic within the stakeholder model.

How, then, can the legitimisation of organisational politics actively be brought forward? It is a daunting question when we think about how the tension between organisational democrati-

sation and the rational model of management runs deep within society as a whole. After all, the language of the rationality applies equally as much to military organisations or religious bodies as it does to Wal-Mart and Microsoft. Church leaders grapple with principles of democratic decision-making processes at the same time as maintaining control over funds and policy. Police forces attempt to be more open and inclusive of minority interest groups within their ranks while operating a command and control approach to management. Charitable organisations rely on voluntary workers, but sometimes try to manage them with the same degree of centralised control found in commercial organisations. The dominance of the rational model is a widespread phenomenon and the movement we can discern towards organisational democracy is but a fraction of the change required.

Education and Political Behaviour

A logical starting point is education. Surely its reach and impact are essential in creating such a massive mindset shift? The answer seems obvious until we remind ourselves that education is anything but value-free. It is an institution that historically has been the central pillar of both democracy and totalitarianism, and while in democratic society education emphasises a plurality of perspectives, it also reinforces the dominant mindset. This is very apparent in management education, which does not exist independently of the prevailing model of effective organisation. In reality it is limited in scope to accelerate the process of legitimising political behaviour, and will remain so until there is a resolute critique of the values that underpin it. Let us look at two major arenas of management education – in-house management training, and business school development programmes – to understand this better.

■ *In-house management training.* In-house training has become a key instrument of human resource policy, often seeking to instil values of organisational consistency and uniformity in management. This can be observed in the emphasis on competency frameworks or psychological profiling that attempt to build conformity of behaviour. It can also be detected in the training that is delivered as part of culture change programmes attempting to implant corporate values and attitudes. Consequently, instead of management training being a vehicle for personal challenge and innovation, it is often viewed with cynicism as another vehicle for top management control. Although more and more is invested in this kind of management training, research shows that much of it has little long-term impact on behaviour. Instead, managers tend to 'surface act', giving the appearance of publicly accepting the ideas presented to them, because they recognise the need to 'play the game' that brings careers, security, and a quiet life.

A significant part of the problem is that too little management training can be considered developmental. By 'developmental' we refer to a process of helping managers consider their own values and attitudes, and how these influence behaviour. Training tends to focus on relatively simple skill transfer or knowledge acquisition, neither of which enables managers to think critically about issues of power and politics. For them to consider alternative models of managing, in-house training would need to take account of the attitudes that influence managers' assumptions about organising. Instead, the focus is usually on specific competencies derived from the rational model, and consequently it does not touch those deep-lying attitudes. Furthermore, managers themselves take the view that time away from the job must be short and relevant, thereby lessening the likelihood that development will be part of the training agenda.

■ *Business school development programmes.* In theory, business school programmes should provide the intellectual critique

absent within the management development curricula of individual organisations. Business schools are university based and
see themselves as thought leaders. However, in reality, they
are caught within the same rational mindset trap as their client
world. Indeed, the academic communities of North America
and Europe have played a substantial role in articulating the
rational model for managers, and it is only recently that
'deviant' theorists have begun to draw attention to the way in
which management literature underemphasises issues of
power and coercion in organisations. The powerful theoretical
conventions built by academia are hard to challenge from
within, and as with most scholarly disciplines, the study of
management and organisation is no exception. Added to this is
the commercial reality of the business schools – they are also
businesses, and they prefer not to alienate their customers. It is
not hard to see how they would find it less risky to teach
within the conventions of the rational model on their
programmes if that is the expectation of the client world.

As with in-house management training, true development
tends not to feature on business school programmes, although
for a different reason. The intellectual predilections of many
business school faculty members lead them to emphasise the
cerebral rather than the emotional domain in their teaching. In
fact, it would not be unfair to say that they can be dismissive
of the 'personal' in development processes, preferring to rely
on the power of ideas to change the thinking of their students.
Managerial attitudes and values are talked about with objec-
tivity and distance rather than addressed from a counselling
perspective. Seminars, presentations and case studies are
preferable to in-depth individual consultations. In other
words, most of the personal development support necessary
for a transformation of mindset is missing in the business
school environment.

In theory, education should provide a vehicle for substantive
progress towards greater organisational democracy. However,

key constituents of the institution of education have become too entangled in the rational model. Too many parts have become aligned to the values of the corporate business mindset, which itself has too much invested in rationality. But there are some signs of change. Academics are increasingly critiquing the processes of management education and the values upon which it is exercised. Similarly there is a growing body of management development specialists and senior managers who are using unconventional and challenging approaches to developing exec-utive talent. Boeing, for instance, commissioned research to identify the extent to which major business schools explicitly discuss 'political savvy' on their executive development programmes, as they identified this as a major managerial capa-bility for their organisation.

Nevertheless, it seems unlikely that there will be any rapid change within education systems sufficient to hasten the democ-ratisation of organisations. Must we then wait for grand scale shifts of values, inching forward as the forces that are changing the business environment take further hold? Of course the answer is 'yes' because we always have to wait for great changes in society. After all, governments come and go, and make little impact on some of the more intractable social problems like the distribution of wealth, or the cycle of deprivation. But do we have to wait as individual managers, responsible for individual organ-isations? Of course not.

Individual Action, Politics and the Art of the Possible

It is in the nature of democratic politics to revere the rightfulness of alternative viewpoints, the ultimate minority view being that of the lone individual voice. Within this core principle lies the means of legitimising organisational politics, and advancing the process of democratisation. For in any business, government agency, charity or ecclesiastical order, it is the determination of individuals and groups to promote their alternative organ-

isational agendas, to act on principled causes, which may serve to dislodge the rational mindset. In other words, within the context of any one organisation, constructive political action can legitimise itself. One only has to look at where progress towards organisational democratisation has been made in particular enterprises to see how this happens. If you doubt that a single person can have an effect on a deeply ingrained and institutionalised rational mindset, think of the impression made by business heroes like Percy Barnevik, the ex-CEO of ABB, Andy Grove of Intel, or Richard Branson of Virgin. They and others like them impact, not just on their own organisations, but on popular consciousness as well. They create organisations that become models for other organisations. And in terms of the power of individual action they are but the tip of the iceberg, for in many circumstances it is possible to find unsung champions of constructive politics who have won widespread respect and admiration for their honourable opposition to ill-conceived corporate policies. Those organisations, or pockets of practice within them, provide glimpses of how truly democratised large-scale organisations might be managed.

ABB has become one such role model for many multinational organisations struggling to come to terms with balancing the opportunities of globalisation with local knowledge and know-how. ABB is known as 1000 companies within one company. It has achieved this by establishing a decorporatised centre of less than 200 staff supporting operations in more than 140 countries. The key to ABB's success lies in the way that decision-making has been radically devolved to each operating unit, while economies of scale are achieved via centralised purchasing, and access to global centres of excellence in different skills and technologies. Internal

benchmarking encourages competition between business units and rewards the best performers.

Underpinning all of this in the early days was Percy Barnevik's drive to make a personal difference, but the organisation's democratised form is now self-sustaining. Barnevik has a strong set of personal values about wanting to contribute to a better world, and was obsessed with developing small entrepreneurial business units, where power and autonomy were pushed to the lowest point. Understanding the divergent views of his organisations was so important to him that, prior to stepping down as CEO, he reckoned he spoke to about 5000 ABB employees every year. He has been labelled as one of the last decade's most visible corporate revolutionaries.

But the impact of individual drive and determination on the democratisation of organisations is not limited to large corporations like ABB or Virgin. Many smaller organisations experiment with radical approaches to managing. For example, at Acer, the personal computer company, Stan Shih, co-founder of the group, has built a federation of self-managing firms held together by mutual interest rather than legal ownership. Some companies are R&D centres, others marketing organisations. Each one is jointly owned by its management and home country investors, with (usually) only a small minority ownership stake held by Acer. In Oticon, a Danish hearing-aid manufacturer, employees choose their own project teams, and these self-managed units have responsibility for the identification and organisation of new business projects. At Semco in Brazil, an example that has captured considerable media attention, Richard Semler has provided an ongoing invitation to production workers to take their operations outside the company and

form their own businesses, with equipment leased from Semco at favourable rates. Again, at UK advertising company St Luke's, they have gone one step further still in terms of democratisation, and the company has become the subject of books, articles and TV programmes around the world.

Andy Law set up St Luke's by taking all the agency staff from the London office of Omnicom, where he had been managing director. All employees at St Luke's are owners, shares being distributed every year in equal proportion to all who have been in the company for the previous year. Law is firmly of the opinion that this ownership increases loyalty, productivity, responsibility, empowerment and trust. Indeed employees have a considerable say in setting their own salaries, this is of course being undertaken with the financial awareness that ownership provides.

Like Percy Barnevik, Law has a strong belief in the idea that small is beautiful. The company is composed of what employees call 'citizen cells' of no more than 35 people, the maximum number, they believe, that can feel a mutual sense of commitment. Trust is generated within these groups because they have a very real operational requirement to work together. Each cell has complete control over its budgets and income streams, and can question from within its direction at any time. There is a warm atmosphere at St Luke's, yet at the same time it is evidently a challenging environment. Individual needs are respected but balanced with organisational agendas. To facilitate this the company pays for all employees to have access to an outside consultant who advises on issues such as careers, relationships, or personality clashes.

These organisations are examples of where individual action from leaders at the top can create organisational democracy. In each case, management has had to find ways of dealing with the realities of conflicting and mutual interests *which have been designed in*. At St Luke's for example, since all employees have more or less equal ownership, there are inevitable differences of opinion about how the business should be run. These differences are managed through a range of formal and informal processes including shareholder days, company days, where all employees discuss the future direction of the business, monthly operational meetings, as well as bar room lobbying.

However, not all organisations are led by enlightened entrepreneurs or radical corporate visionaries, so what are the possibilities for individual action by managers working from less favourable organisational starting points – most managers, in other words?

The Beginnings of an Agenda for Personal Action

Personal action that either supports or competes with the agendas of others arises because individuals see it as worthwhile. Political behaviour for its own sake can be no more than a game, a form of deviant organisational activity disconnected from relationships and meaningful work. Being political is not an end in itself but a means to an end, and most of us will engage in politics only when there is personal gain to be had. And as we have tried to show throughout this book, for political action to be constructive, personal gain must be in the service of others, not just self-seeking. Worthy causes are the key, whatever your own organisational starting point.

Maybe you already have one – most managers do. It is probably not far out of reach if you cannot produce your personal manifesto right at this moment. Just remind yourself of the ambitions you have for your team, or what you would like your part of the business to achieve. Think of how much your professional

values mean to you, or how important your specialist knowledge is to your colleagues, clients and suppliers. Ask yourself (again) about the mistaken strategic decisions taken by others on behalf of you and the business, or the neglect of huge opportunities in your markets. What about all those frustrations you have some-times felt because obvious organisational improvements never happen? Just one item from the last off-site workshop 'wish list' may be all you need. Consider but one of these suggestions and you will soon find your worthy cause. In fact you will probably be spoilt for choice. And if you want to make that cause a direct assault on rational management thinking – think carefully. There is plenty of scope but you do need to be circumspect about directness. But you could contemplate some of the following:

- Challenging your management development professionals to explain why they are trying to build conformity of behaviour at a time when diversity provides the basis for innovation and creativity.

- Coaching those who work for you to question assumptions about corporate unity. Even better, do the same with colleagues who do not work for you, like your boss. Call it 'scenario painting' or 'brain-storming', not coaching. Remember how much language matters.

- Recruiting and nurturing organisational misfits so that they blossom into leaders of pockets of good practice. Protecting the pockets once they begin to take shape, and until they can stand on their own success.

- Suggesting to your HRM people that political skills should be included in their competency framework, and that they should reconsider the value of team development for the organisation.

- Asking senior management if they would like you to lead a special project to evaluate the benefits of radical approaches to employee ownership and rewards.

■ Tasking business school academics and consultants with whom you come into contact to show how their models of management and organisation challenge top managers, not merely support their assumptions.

Each of these agendas alone may appear insignificant. But in the context of your own organisation they provide a point of departure in legitimising politics, and individual action is axiomatic in this process. Progress is made by exploiting the loopholes and contradictions of the rational model from within that model, and whatever the worthwhile cause, the power and benefit of constructive political behaviour can only really be appreciated when experienced in practice.

So are you convinced? We hope that you are, but perhaps for some, the risks of constructive political activity may still seem too great. If that is your own conclusion, do pause one more time. For constructive political action provides you with the opportunity to take greater self-control, to see choices and alternative courses of action, and to realise causes that are worthwhile for you and for others. And remember this also. The rational model of organising has been around for several centuries, yet in the last ten years we have begun to witness an unfreezing of organising principles that 50 years ago might have seemed unthinkable. Like it or not, organisational forms are changing significantly, perhaps fundamentally. How long will it be before truly democratised organisations, built on principles of constructive political behaviour, become realities? Why wait to find out when you can be ahead of the game? After all as a good manager, that is where you would want to be.

Index